D1597723

SOUL OF WILDERNESS

SOUL OF WILDERNESS

Mountain Journeys in Western BC and Alaska

JOHN BALDWIN AND LINDA BILY

HARBOUR PUBLISHING

CONTENTS

Page 1: This striking granite spire rises from a ridge in the middle of the Homathko Icefield. The upper part of the spire is a solid block of granite. *Linda Bily (LB)*

Pages 2–3: The view south from a camp on the Homathko Icefield. *LB*

This spread: Heavy mineralization has produced this dazzling spectrum of colours in Sluice Creek in the South Chilcotin Mountains. *LB*

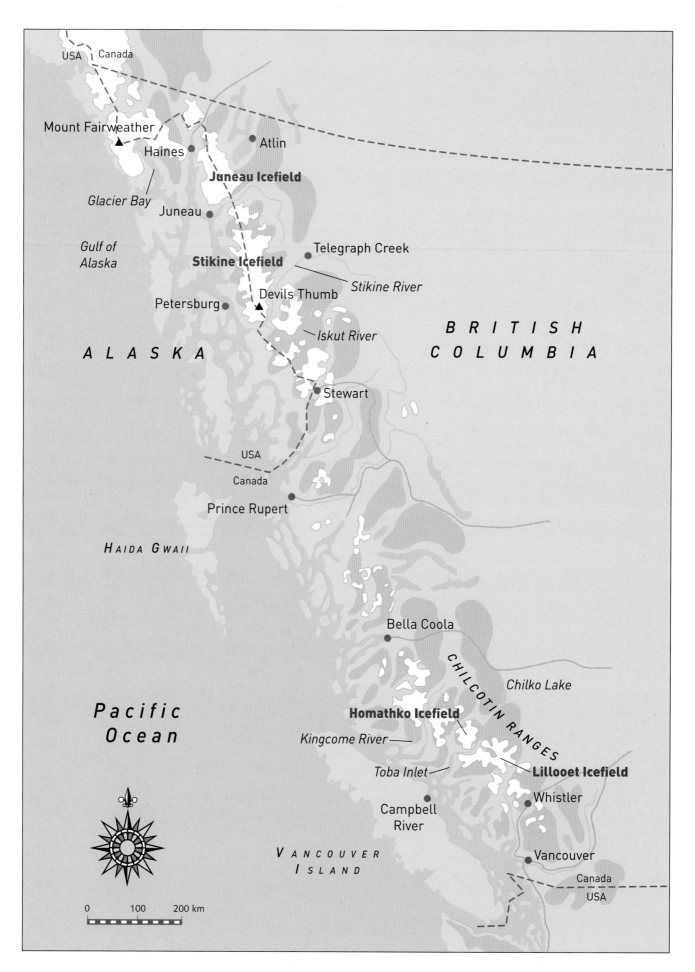

INTRODUCTION:
FOOTSTEPS IN THE WILDERNESS

Most of us exist for most of the time in worlds which are humanly arranged, themed and controlled. One forgets that there are environments which do not respond to the flick of a switch or the twist of a dial, and which have their own rhythms and orders of existence.

—Robert Macfarlane

"Wilderness" is one of those vague concepts. Most people have an idea of what it is, but defining it is difficult. The root of the word implies that wilderness is an area that remains in its natural state, uninhabited and uncultivated. But what does that mean? Does it include the patch of trees behind your backyard? How big an area do you need for something to count as wilderness? Can you see wilderness from a road or an airplane?

We are fortunate to live near the western mountains of British Columbia, which contain some of the last wilderness in North America outside of the Arctic. The mountains are home to grizzly bears and wolves, and where salmon run wild and mountain goats and wolverines roam through terrain that has not changed since the arrival of Europeans to North America. This book is a look at those wilderness areas: their beauty, their essence, their soul.

But why wilderness? What is it that draws us to wilderness? In the eyes of Western society, wilderness, by definition, excludes man—it is something outside our culture. But in other cultures around the world, wilderness is nature, which is seen as home. Where did our connection to Mother Earth go? How can we bring wilderness back into our culture?

Following pages: Descending to an azure blue lake in Sockeye Creek.

John Baldwin (JB)

7

The distant peak of Haymaker Mountain framed by an alpine tarn. *JB*

Opposite: Peter Paré cools off in the spray from a waterfall below Mount Alfred. *JB*

Pages 12–13: On a ski traverse of the Homathko Icefield, we explore an extraordinary ice tunnel formed by a crevasse near the summit of Mount Cradock (see chapter 1). *LB*

The existence of large areas of wilderness in the mountains of British Columbia is not due to the foresight of our grandfathers. These tracts of alpine rock and ice escaped collision with Western culture only because of their inhospitable nature. But today, with increasing population and development, the pressures on this globally significant wilderness are enormous. Do we have a responsibility to protect it?

In this modern world, where it is estimated that 75 percent of the earth's ice-free land mass owes its appearance to humans, how many people have ever been somewhere they couldn't see a road, a building or another person? How many people have ever truly experienced wilderness?

We would like to share our experiences from over forty years in the mountains of western British Columbia. This is not the only example of wilderness left on our planet but it is special to us as it is part of our home. We have been drawn to its spectacular landscapes and have ventured into its deep valleys and climbed high onto its icy mountaintops. In this book we describe our journeys and bring you face to face with this exceptional region.

The journeys are mountaineering trips on foot and on skis and are a sampling of some of the more recent forays we have enjoyed together. Most are typically one to three weeks long and involve travel across pristine mountain terrain where it's pretty much guaranteed that you won't see anybody, and there are no signs of human existence at all. Ours are not heart-stopping tales of conquest and hardship, however. The purpose of our trips is simply to see as many of these special places as we can—to wander across high meadows, climb to and ski from mountain summits, and revel in the magic of wilderness. When asked why we do these trips we sometimes reply half-jokingly that "It's so beautiful, someone has to go look at it."

Queen's cup flowers carpet a trail through lush rainforest. *JB*

Above: Phil Hammer's silhouette adds scale to the impressive north side of Bute Mountain in the distance. *LB*

Left: Scrambling up the final summit ridge of Saint John Peak on the Homathko Icefield. *JB*

Following pages: Brian Sheffield skis pristine powder slopes below Mount Thiassi. *LB*

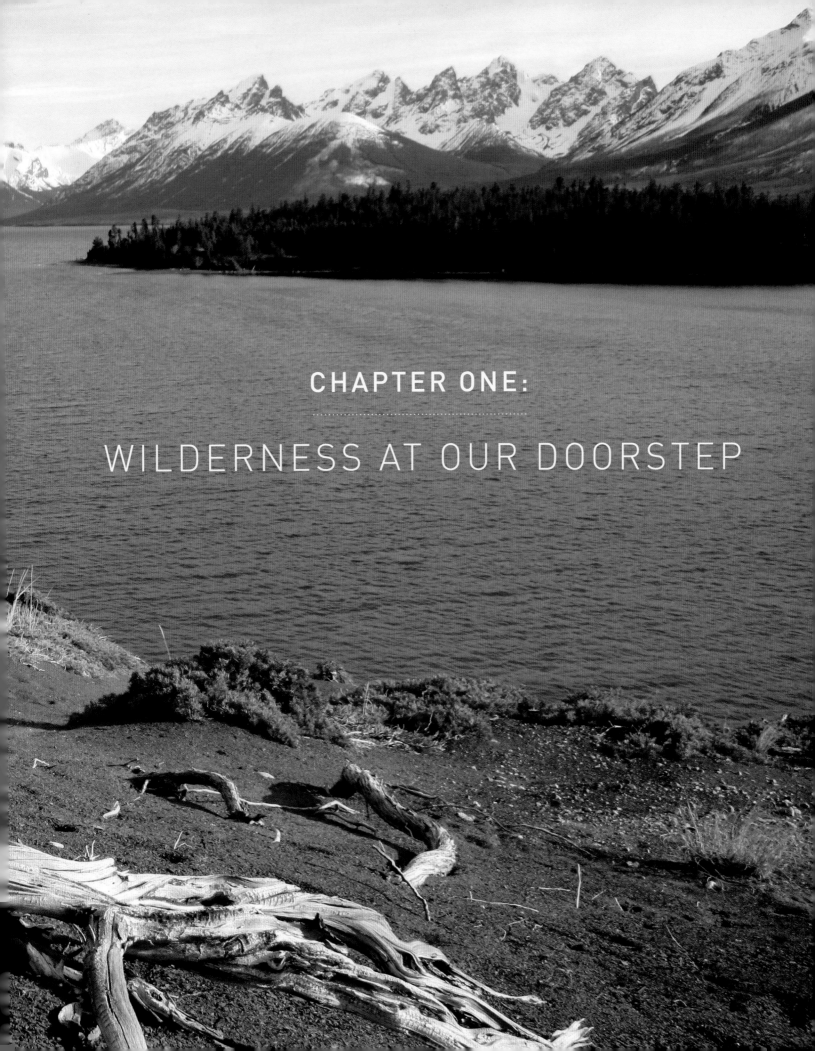

CHAPTER ONE:

WILDERNESS AT OUR DOORSTEP

Climb the mountains and get their good tidings. Nature's peace will flow into you as sunshine flows into trees. The winds will blow their own freshness into you, and the storms their energy, while cares will drop off like autumn leaves.

—John Muir

Previous pages: View south down Chilko Lake from the Nemaia valley. *JB*

Aerial view of the Homathko Icefield. The icefield is about 60 km across. Our ski route travels across the icefield from Chilko Lake in the back right to Bute Inlet at bottom left. *JB*

We stood on the shore of Chilko Lake, loading our skis onto Roland Class's water taxi. Anxious to take advantage of the glassy calm water, Roland gestured for us to hurry. Scrambling on board, we headed south down the long ribbon of turquoise water, gawking at the jagged peaks rising abruptly on both sides of the lake. The largest high-elevation lake in BC, Chilko Lake is the inland equivalent of a coastal fjord and runs 65 km back into the mountains from the high, rolling Chilcotin Plateau. Roland dropped us off on a white sand beach in a sheltered bay near the mouth of Farrow Creek. It was the end of April 2014, and our skis seemed out of place. With the warm sun and the sapphire blue water, we felt like we had just been transported to a beach in the tropics. But the surrounding snowy summits reminded us what we were there for.

Together with our friends Diana Diaconu, Gord Ferguson, Stan Sovdat and Phil

Hammer, we planned to climb high into the mountains and spend three weeks skiing across the interconnected glaciers that form the Homathko Icefield. Perched in the mountains between the southwest shore of Chilko Lake on the east and Bute Inlet on the west, the Homathko Icefield is a vast wilderness area. Yet it is less than 250 km from our home in Vancouver. This is roughly the same as the distance from Boston to New York—imagine if there was a wilderness area the size of Switzerland a mere 250 km from New York. It is a wilderness at our doorstep.

Carrying five days' food, we strapped our skis to our packs and started walking up Farrow Creek. We followed a rough trail through the mossy forest floor. The trail soon became fainter and interrupted by lots of deadfall. Weaving our skis through the deadfall was slow, hard work. Phil livened the mood with, "There may be lots of deadfall but at least there are mosquitos." In the hopes of finding easier terrain we headed for the creek. In 1994 a glacier-dammed lake at the head of Farrow Creek had burst and a huge outwash flood, known as a jökulhlaup, had rushed down the valley, taking out large swaths of forest along the banks of the creek. The walking was much easier on the gravel bars but to get to them we needed to constantly wade across the creek in our ski boots. Views opened up as we moved up the creek, and we set up our first camp on a wide gravel bar. Relaxing in the evening sun with the rock faces of Mount Merriam towering above us on one side and the steep avalanche-strewn slopes of Mount Farrow on the other, civilization felt a long way away. We at last felt like we had entered the wilderness.

Walking along the shore of Chilko Lake to Farrow Creek on our first day of the Homathko Icefield ski traverse. *LB*

Opposite page: Gord Ferguson peers down through a hole in the snow bridge over the crevasse we discovered just below the summit of Mount Cradock. The crevasse was open on both ends and formed a tunnel. *LB*

John crosses a log over Farrow Creek. *LB*

By the next afternoon we reached snow and eagerly put on our skis. We crossed the toe of the glacier at the head of the valley and camped near a small lake at treeline. There we dug out the first of two food caches we had flown in by helicopter prior to our trip. As we cooked dinner we spotted two goats gazing down at us from a bluff, and later a grizzly bear came ambling through the pass, staying above us to avoid our camp. That night the drumming sounds of a grouse and the rolling hoots of an owl lulled us to sleep.

A weak storm moved in the next morning. Rather than continuing our trek we hung out in the valley with the hopes of getting a clear day to ski up Mount Cradock (2,825 m). Light snow and wind filled the air. If we were up high on a glacier we would have been pinned down in a snowstorm, but at treeline in the sheltered valley it was peaceful. We made short ski trips down the valley to explore the area and gradually settled into the rhythm of the place.

After two days the wind calmed down and a clear night brought us a gorgeous day. We set off early in the crisp air up the Goddard Glacier, passing by brightly lit seracs. The gentle glacier curved gradually westward to where the summit pyramid rose steeply from it. The opportunity to ski up the high peaks in such a remote place is one of the highlights of these long traverses.

We switchbacked our way up through a few crevasses and crossed to north-facing slopes. Less than 100 m from the summit we stumbled upon a wall of blue ice where the glacier had pulled away from the upper slope. The wall of ice led into the bottom of a crevasse that was filled in with snow, and we were able to ski in between parallel walls of pale blue ice several storeys high. The top of the crevasse was covered with a snow bridge, which had a hole in it that formed a natural skylight. But as we looked around we realized that the covered crevasse was actually open on the other end and formed a tunnel about 100 m long. We took turns skiing onto the roof of the tunnel and peering down at the others below.

We continued to the summit of Mount Cradock. We took our skis off and kicked steps up the final steep slope to the narrow ridge of snow forming the peak. There we had our first bird's-eye view of the landscape. To the east, where we started, a slice of Chilko Lake glimmered between high rocky peaks. To the west, in the direction we were headed, the entire Homathko Icefield was spread out across the horizon, and we could pick out the peaks and glaciers we would ski past in the next few weeks.

From the summit, the 1,300 m descent to our camp turned out to be a fabulous run. We started off by skiing a long north-facing stretch of powder snow, then made fast turns weaving around some crevasses, then hit a long mellow section and finally soft corn snow past the main icefall and down into camp. We leap-frogged each other all the way down with ear-to-ear grins.

Feeling rewarded by our exhilarating side trip up Mount Cradock, we were happy to pack up camp the next day and continue on our traverse. Now, with heavier loads from our food cache, we used our collapsible toboggans made from kids' plastic crazy carpets to lessen the load on our backs. Still carrying our big packs, we dragged

Opposite page: Linda descends Saint John Peak with Mount Grenville visible in the far distance across Homathko Icefield. *JB*

Below: Stan Sovdat on the summit of Mount Cradock. *JB*

Below right: Ski tracks glisten in spring corn snow. *JB*

Pages 26–27: A view of our camp near Mount Grenville with Mount Waddington, the highest peak in BC, in the background. *LB*

the crazy carpet "boggies" behind us loaded with some of the food. We headed down the gentle valley floor of Boulanger Creek. Our camp had been on the watershed between coastal and interior drainages: Farrow Creek drains to Chilko Lake and the interior, while Boulanger Creek feeds into the Southgate River and drains directly to the coast. As we moved down the valley we started to feel the coastal influence. It is rare to see such dramatic changes in such a short distance, but in just 6 km we left behind the stunted alpine fir and pine trees typical of the interior and entered coastal stands of solid mountain hemlock draped in lichen. Several goats watched us from high up on steep granite slabs. We camped in the upper Southgate River valley beside a clump of stunted mountain hemlocks. The valley appeared to be a major animal thoroughfare to drier inland valleys, as we spotted more than half a dozen wolverine and grizzly bear tracks.

On Day 7 we left the tents set up and headed off on another side trip to an isolated, unnamed 2,530 m summit on the divide between the Southgate River and Deschamps Creek, which flows into Chilko Lake at Franklyn Arm. More panoramic views of the Homathko Icefield were on offer, but this time we could also see all the way down the Southgate River, which lines the eastern side of the icefield. The valley deepens as it makes its way to the coast, and where the Southgate turns west under the huge peaks of Raleigh and Gilbert it is walled in by an impressive 3,000 m of relief.

The ski run back to camp was even better than Cradock and we swooped down the silky corn snow with views of Franklyn Arm behind. That evening we enjoyed

our dinner in the warm sun beside the stunted hemlock trees. Spring was in the air and the valley was full of small birds migrating north.

A sun dog indicated a change in the weather, but Day 8 started out clear and we followed fresh grizzly bear tracks up the gentle valley. The bear walked pigeon-toed and left paw prints sunk deeply into the soft snow. We skied through the pass and down the other side, forced below treeline for a short stretch before heading up through a canyon on Deschamps Creek, which opened up onto a flat meadow surrounded by peaks. We camped in a cluster of trees as it started snowing, and it snowed lightly overnight and all the next day. As we needed good weather to navigate over the next part of our route, we took a rest day, lazing and napping in the tent, listening to the *cluck-cla-cla* of white-tailed ptarmigan.

The next day we travelled west over Nine Mile Ridge, down to Allaire Creek and finally ascended onto the northeast corner of the Homathko Icefield. We left behind the sheltered interior valleys and ventured out onto the expansive glaciers that make up the icefield. The icefield welcomed us with an exhilarating side trip to Saint John

Below: View out the tent door from our camp on the north edge of the Homathko Icefield. *JB*

Peak (2,774 m). We left our packs on the flat névé, skied up a steep chute, and then scrambled up a narrow rock ridge to the final summit. We took turns standing on the tiny mountaintop, staring at the expanse of wild peaks jutting out of the icefield, with all but their summits drowned in ice. By the time we were ready to leave the peak, the sun had softened the steep icy chute we ascended and it made for a fabulous silky run back to our packs. We camped that night at our second food cache and reloaded our supplies. Fresh potato stew, canned fruit and beer put smiles on our faces.

We were surprised the next morning by lowering clouds. It snowed lightly all day as we felt our way south across the gentle glaciers in dense fog to near Reed Peak. Occasional glimpses of rock outcrops helped us navigate the otherwise grey landscape. The poor visibility made the huge expanse of the icefield seem even larger. It's unnerving to ski across a wide expanse of snow without any visual reference. The only way to tell how fast you are moving in the fog is to let your ski pole drag in the snow.

The next morning we continued in the mist, skiing by feel and guided by a compass. At lunch the clouds lifted and we discovered we were sitting under a crooked granite pinnacle jutting out of the icefield. The clearing continued in the afternoon but there were still ominous-looking clouds in the distance behind Mount Waddington. We camped near Mount Grenville (3,079 m), the highest peak on the icefield, hoping the weather would be good enough the next day for us to ski up the peak.

Day 14 the weather was cooperating. We awoke to stunning views of the massive peaks of the Waddington Range. We grabbed our daypacks and headed towards Mount Grenville. A ramp led through the first icefall to the upper bench below a massive blue ice bulge hanging off Grenville's steep north face. We switchbacked up the bowl east of the summit and crossed a bergschrund to gain the summit ridge. A narrow notch that dropped steeply on both sides was just passable with skis on, and a bit of boot packing led to the final summit. With wispy clouds blowing past across the blue skies, the views were intermittent. But this seemed to make the glimpses of the entire Homathko Icefield even more awe-inspiring. The first few turns on our descent felt especially wild as the rugged terrain around us drifted in and out of view. Nice turns in the upper part of the bowl ended with some grabby snow that caught everyone by surprise, and below it was an extraordinary pitch carving turns under some blue seracs. We love the feeling of the long, slow glide back to camp—it seems to make us feel even smaller than when we are walking. We ate dinner while the evening sun turned the slopes of Grenville crimson, and at dusk a full moon rose just left of the peak. The night was absolutely still and quiet and we slept like babies.

A raven woke us up to a clear morning. We headed southwest on the last stretch of icefield, which took us onto a narrow glaciated ridge leading over to Bute Mountain. As we skied along the ridge, the scent of the forest wafted up from the deep coastal valleys and we could see and hear a 150 m high waterfall that was 2,000 m below us in the Teaquahan River valley. All day we were treated to stunning views of the snow-capped north face of Mount Bute, and at the end of the day we camped under

Opposite bottom: At the end of our long descent from Mount Grenville, Diana Diaconu steers around a crevasse, with Mount Bute in the distance. *LB*

Pages 30–31: A lone skier descends below the looming ice bulge on the north side of Mount Grenville. *JB*

John strolls along slabs of bare rock next to the Bute Glacier. From this vantage point we were able to examine our route off the glacier and down to Galleon Creek. *LB*

the towering face—but only after having to down climb a steep, mushy snow slope next to a big icefall. All night long we heard the gurgle of water running down the cliff at the edge of the glacier.

Day 16 was again clear and we attempted one last side trip to ski up Mount Bute (2,804 m). It was also our hundredth day of skiing for the winter. The route was complicated and required climbing over a high col and traversing across steep slopes to reach the south side of the mountain. At the first col we realized that the hot sun was already affecting the steep slopes ahead and the threat of avalanches was too high to continue. We skied to a nearby col for a view before retreating back to camp. We spent the afternoon lounging below camp on sun-warmed rock slabs adjacent to where the glacier drops off into Galleon Creek. It was a spectacular spot, with wrinkled waves of blue seracs jutting out of the snowy glacier right next to the slabs and the imposing north face of Mount Bute rising above us on the other side of the glacier. We could also see down our exit route to Galleon Creek and made mental notes of the difficult terrain that lay ahead. Melted out of the snow above the slabs was a heather- and lichen-covered outcrop with some running water. We splashed ourselves clean and rinsed our socks. It was warm against the rock and we enjoyed hanging out and soaking up the energy of this amazing place.

It rained all night and was foggy in the morning. We packed up as the fog began to lift. The exit into Galleon Creek was a wild adventure. We skied down a narrow trough next to walls of towering seracs and blue ice, made even more impressive by the rain and mist. Once we got below the glacier, cliffs forced us left and we followed benches past several waterfalls across to the base of the enormous granite walls of Mount Bute. Near-vertical slabs of rock rose 1,900 m above us to the summit. It is one of the largest rock faces in the Coast Mountains. Craning our necks to see the upper pitches of rock, it was hard to grasp how gigantic the face is.

Our snow ran out at the base of the rock face and we were forced to carry our skis into thick bush. Wrestling with slide alder and devil's club made the travelling slow. At one point we had to cross the icy cold waist-deep Galleon Creek. But in some ways

the difficulties only served to make the ruggedness of the wild valley even more astounding. In the midst of the thick bush, lemon-hued monkey flowers were starting to blossom and lower down we stumbled onto an open swampy meadow covered in bright yellow skunk cabbage, with the cliffs of Mount Bute as a towering backdrop. We camped that night by the creek and dried our socks beside a big fire.

As we moved down the valley the next day we picked up a rough trail. Open mossy stretches of the old-growth forest were interrupted by many slide paths, where we would lose the trail in tangled webs of slide alder and willow. The only prints on the trail were grizzly bear tracks. Near the end of the valley we picked up an old logging road. The road was partially overgrown but led

Linda is dwarfed by a grove of giant cedar trees during our hike down Galleon Creek to Bute Inlet. *JB*

down to a logging camp on the banks of the Homathko River, the end point for our trip. The humid coastal valley seemed a long way from the sunny shores of Chilko Lake. We were all tired from our journey, but inside we were filled with the energy of all the awe-inspiring places we experienced along our route.

We spent a day lounging around camp, absorbing the rugged Homathko River valley and talking to camp caretakers Chuck, Sheron and Wayne. The lush green of the coast and the sound of running water everywhere were a bewildering contrast to the starkness of the icefield we had just come from. We also spotted four grizzlies around the camp.

Our trip ended on Day 20 with a water taxi ride down Bute Inlet to Campbell River. Sitting in the boat, it felt strange to be moving without any effort. Dark green mountainsides and slabs of rock rose for almost 3,000 m to the surrounding peaks. In Campbell River our ski boots and ski pants attracted stares, as everyone had switched to shorts and sandals for that sunny day at the end of May. We looked and felt like aliens. A few people stopped and asked us where we had just come back from, but there was no way to describe our three weeks in the wilderness in a few sentences.

Pages 34–35: John looks out at the ridges lining the Kingcome River valley. *LB*

CHAPTER TWO:

WHERE THE RIDGES RUN WILD

When I'm away from this tall, never-tamed country, I ache to be
back within its folds the way other folks miss home.
—Douglas Chadwick

Opposite page: Peter Paré and Lisa Baile stand beyond an arch formed by a disintegrating crevasse. *LB*

Below: Most skyline traverses in the Coast Mountains start from one of the long dark coastal inlets that penetrate far back into the mountains. Our trip along the ridges above Seymour Inlet started by being dropped off by a float plane on Owikeeno Lake, shown here. *JB*

The Great Skyline Traverses of the Coast Mountains

The western edge of the Coast Mountains where the big icefields spill off into the deep coastal valleys is a rugged band of wilderness that stretches north from Vancouver. Thousands of square kilometres of mountains are stacked up against each other as far as the eye can see. Buried deep within this wilderness are dozens of alpine ridge systems snaking their way through the rugged terrain. They are a unique bit of geography not found elsewhere in the Coast Mountains and seldom found in other mountain ranges. Usually mountain ridge tops are difficult to traverse, but these high coastal ridge systems define alpine routes that can be travelled on foot with relative ease for two to three weeks or more. Rounded ridge tops perched high in the sky are completely separated from deep U-shaped valleys by thousands of metres of cliffs, slabs, waterfalls and steep forest. These are the great skyline traverses of the Coast Mountains.

Top: Aerial view of the meandering Toba River emptying into Toba Inlet. *JB*

Above: John ascends a snowfield covered in sun cups. *LB*

Opposite: John peers across Lahlah Creek towards a jumbled icefall descending from an unnamed peak. *LB*

The scenery is in your face every step of the way and it is a bit like being on the summit of a mountain for the entire trip. These ridge tops are made of never-ending slabs of smooth granite—in many places so extensive that it seems like the whole trip is on one solid piece of rock. Typically these traverses are each about 100 km in length and involve 7,000 m or more of total elevation gain (not counting side trips). The best time of year for these trips is usually midsummer.

We are lucky to share a year-round passion for exploring the wilderness and mountains together, and have found others who share it as well. Beginning in 2003 we spent four summers with Lisa Baile and Peter Paré traversing the ridge systems near Seymour Inlet, Kingcome Inlet, Toba Inlet and Jervis Inlet. The photographs shown are from this series of skyline traverses, while the text that follows describes a particular trip to the high divides above the Kingcome River.

The Search for the Perfect Tarn

If you run to your bookshelf and pull out your 1983 *Canadian Alpine Journal*, you'll find a five-page article brimming with spectacular photographs of the rugged divide between the Kingcome and Satsalla Rivers. Narrow, snow-covered ridges snaking off into the distance, valleys walled in by thousands of metres of granite cliffs, tumbling icefalls and horn-shaped peaks. You would think the Satsalla Divide would have caught someone's eye in the twenty-two years since that article appeared. But in 2004 no one had been there since John Clarke and Jamie Sproule travelled the length of it in 1977. With plans to complete a summer horseshoe traverse around the Kingcome River, which would retrace John and Jamie's route, the four of us flew in to the Satsalla Divide at the beginning of August 2004, placing two food caches to the north and west on the way.

Our initial camp was high on the ridges east of Lahlah Creek. We enjoyed our first dinner sprawled on slabs of rock, peering into the depths of the surrounding valleys that defined the ridges we were going to be travelling on. The Satsalla River valley is particularly rugged and scenic. A muddy glacial lake at the snout of the Satsalla Glacier lay 1,700 m below us, with cliffs rising 2,000 m from its shores to the peaks on the far side of the valley. No amount of planning and staring at maps before a trip can prepare you for views like this. The anticipation and dreaming were over—and we were ecstatic.

After a side trip south along the ridge on the first day, we packed north along the narrow divide the second day, climbing over a 2,133 m summit where we added our names to the scrap of paper John and Jamie had left in a cairn twenty-seven years earlier. After lunch on the peak, we quickly discovered the reason for a strong east wind as wispy cirrus and lenticular clouds began to fill the sky. By evening we were struggling to set up the tents in driving rain 10 km to the north—but not before we had been treated to wild views of the huge icefalls on the north side of unnamed Peak 2,133 m. Rain pelted loudly on the tent all night but eventually subsided in the morning, and we set off side-hilling across steep glaciers high above the stunning S-turn

Pages 40–41: A group of climbers ascends the glacier towards the summit of Mount John Clarke. *LB*

Right: Peter Paré blends in with the crevassed glacier behind. *JB*

Below: Pink monkey flowers grow in a wet area overlooking the Kingcome Glacier. *JB*

made by the Satsalla Glacier. At the edge of the Ha-iltzuk Icefield, we made a side trip to Peak 2,316 m, where the clouds periodically ripped open to offer us amazing views to the valley glacier below. We continued onto and across the icefield in the afternoon, staggering like drunken sailors as we stumbled over and around enormous sun cups.

Hoping to have sweeping views down the Kingcome River, we had planned to circle around the head of the river by climbing past Mount Kinch on the edge of the Ha-iltzuk Icefield. But rain, wet snow and near whiteout conditions set in. Rather than wait it out, we set off confidently with Peter's new GPS. Ironically, the only time one of us put our foot in a crevasse was when John was concentrating so hard on following the GPS that he forgot to look up. We arrived at our food cache west of Mount Kinch cold and wet and wondering if summer was over.

Our friend John Clarke used to tell everyone that you could do most of these ridge traverses with your hands in your pockets. While it is true that long sections are straightforward walking on snow, heather or slabs of smooth rock, the real truth is that you will need an ice axe in your hand the entire trip. This is general mountaineering, not backpacking. One of the traverses around the Tahumming River at the head of Toba Inlet is described by Andy Selters in *Ways to the Sky: A Historical Guide to North American Mountaineering*: "Technical climbing challenges are modest, but the demands of logistics, extensive alpine travel, the stormy climate and essentially no opportunity for escape make this a scenic, high value engagement." It is given a French climbing grade of "Difficult"—the same grade as the West Buttress of Denali. Route planning is key.

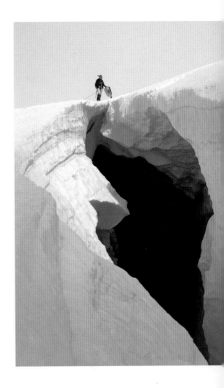

Lisa Baile poses on a snow bridge over a deep crevasse. *LB*

Goats ramble easily on steep rocky ground. *LB*

The other thing that happens is that because these traverses generally lack any kind of escape route, they provide the same sense of purpose as an expedition to climb a major peak. However, since the technical challenges are modest and the traverses lack any major objective, there is a tendency for the focus to shift away from the climbing difficulties and be replaced by the opportunity to simply enjoy the rugged wilderness.

We pushed on in bad weather the next day as well, hoping to reach the lush meadows and tarns further along our route if it cleared up. It turned out to be just as wet and cold as the day before, but our packs were heavier with the added food from the food cache and we had some difficulty descending a steep, crevassed slope north of Peak 2,256 m. The following day was brighter as we continued south onto a promontory above the Kingcome River valley. We lunched amongst a few small flowers clinging to the top of a volcanic pinnacle, and soaked up the tangled view of ridges and valleys snaking off into the distance. Below us the branches of the Kingcome Glacier converged into a jumble of blue seracs, which plunged deep into the forest.

The ridges above Princess Louisa Inlet were sculpted by glaciers to form these spectacular rock patterns. *LB*

The second half of our trip followed the high spine of mountains down the west side of the Kingcome River. Since we were sticking almost entirely to narrow ridge tops surrounded by deep coastal valleys, cols or passes were actually low points along our route. The first broad pass between Catto Creek and the Kingcome River turned out to be an extraordinary place of lush heather meadows dotted with tarns and lakes—rare in this part of the Coast Mountains.

Our first unclimbed peak of the trip was the 2,100 m summit west of McFee Creek. The peak is offset from the main divide and we discovered that the only way to get to it was to traverse across the middle of a big cliff on narrow, exposed grassy ledges used by goats. A short step in the north ridge involved a bit of rock scrambling. We rushed back to our packs in the evening light and set up camp amongst pools of water and trickling streams on polished slabs of rock perched high above the glacier on the southwest side of a 1,900 m dome.

Our second major pass to descend into was the narrow col between Powley Creek and McFee Creek. The col is surrounded by granite cliffs and slabs, and it took us most of the day to descend 600 m down a damp gully to get to it. Near the bottom of the gully, we found ourselves on a bench with bluffs below us on all sides. Even though we found some bear droppings there, we could not find an easy way down and were forced to do a rappel at the bottom of the gully. The descent was very hot, so the whole way down we were looking forward to the tarns we had spotted in the col. These turned out to be some of the best tarns we had swam in yet, including a 70 m long pool set into a small granite cliff and surrounded by sun-warmed slabs. We spent the rest of the afternoon washing clothes and swimming. While we were eating dinner we watched a black bear cross the pass.

The climb south out of the col had looked a bit tricky from a distance, but it went fairly easily the next day; after another swim at lunch we continued to Peak 2,195 m. This is the highest peak on the west side of the Kingcome River. The peak turned out to be a fun scramble from the south, and we built a big cairn on top while soaking up the views. We could almost see our entire traverse spread out like a horseshoe around us, from our start on the Satsalla Divide, to our route across the edge of the icefield, and finally the rest of our ridge system snaking off to the south.

Our second food cache was just south of the peak, so we eagerly rushed down to our buckets sitting on the snow. Upon reaching them, however, we realized that our one and only can of white gas was missing. After some searching we figured out that it had slid on the snow and plummeted over a 150 m cliff. While watching a crimson sunset, we deliberated over what to do about our predicament. We decided to abandon all our soup and tea, figuring we could manage as long as we could find some firewood for at least one night.

After the food cache, we continued southeast on ridges that led around the headwaters of the Atwaykellesse River. This was granite country and there were impressive cliffs and slabs everywhere. We started to see more and more pools of water lying on the ridge tops. Shortly after passing fresh grizzly bear prints on the glacier,

Pages 46–47: Peter Paré and Lisa Baile air dry after a swim in a small tarn high above Toba Inlet. *LB*

The Satsalla Glacier snakes its way down into the deep valley of the Satsalla River. *LB*

we dropped to a flat section of the ridge at about 1,600 m, where we discovered an especially alluring tarn with several arms and bays. We jumped into the pool and ran around on the slabs in our bare feet.

There were several more inviting tarns further along the ridge, and it was late in the day by the time we reached the 1,830 m peak west of the lake at the head of the Atwaykellesse River. Because we were low on white gas, we continued down the other side towards the narrow pass between the Atwaykellesse and Kingcome Rivers. About 200 m above the pass, we came onto a sloping shoulder of rock above the lake, where we camped on smooth slabs beside yet another tarn. Some dead trees from avalanche debris gave us just enough firewood for the night.

In the morning we continued down to the pass below at 1,100 m. Clear streams of water meandered through green subalpine meadows walled in by huge, curving cliffs. The full heat of summer was upon us as we had our first swim of the day in the small lake just east of the pass. On the climb out of the pass, we swung around to the south side of the long, bald nose of rock rising to the southeast. We got separated from Lisa and Peter as we tried to work out routes through the steep slabs and cliffs. Eventually, we broke out onto gentler slabs with more tarns at 1,400 m. This was such an enticing spot that we frolicked around the tarn long enough to sunburn our bums.

We discovered yet another beautiful tarn at 1,600 m and were caught diving into it by Lisa and Peter, who had bypassed us on their route up the ridge and were looking down on us from the peak above. With this many tarns, we were hardly even

getting sweaty between swims. The 1,707 m peak gave tremendous views of the deep Kingcome valley walled in by cliffs and slabs, and we could see the pointy spire of Haymaker Mountain rising above the Satsalla River in the distance. We continued south from the peak on smooth waves of polished granite slabs. About 1 km south of the peak, we crested a small rise to see Peter and Lisa both lying naked, basking on a sun-warmed slab beside a perfectly round tarn. It seemed that the goal of our trip had shifted from climbing mountains to searching for tarns.

The next day, we continued south along the divide for 10 km. As we travelled at 1,800 m with steep slopes plunging to sea level on both sides, this section felt a bit like hiking through the sky. Peter and Lisa had set off early, and we had promised to limit ourselves to only four swims so as not to get too far behind. We were squeaky clean when we caught up to them at our last camp, on the east shoulder of the 1,829 m peak above Mason Creek. Peter remarked that we should call our trip "The Search for the Perfect Tarn."

On our last day we had 4 km of ridge to travel before the divide ended abruptly at the junction of the Clear and Kingcome Rivers. With time running out, we chose our remaining swims carefully. Our search for the perfect tarn was over when we climbed past the last summit and saw what lay ahead. Long, sloping slabs led down

and across to a bald granite dome a kilometre away at the end of the ridge. The sides of the dome plunged 1,200 m into the deep, green Kingcome valley on three sides. Perched on top and surrounded by smooth slabs was a large deep green pool where house-sized blocks of solid granite formed islands in the clear water.

While swimming, there was an unobstructed 360-degree view of the surrounding mountains. We lost track of how many times we alternated between the cool water and the sun-baked rock. We have never been so clean at the end of fifteen days in the mountains. It was a fitting end to our trip. We were picked up late in the afternoon by helicopter and flown back to Port McNeill.

Trips like this are absolutely breathtaking, but we have always been surprised by how seldom any of these high-ridge traverses between inlets are done. It would be a shame if another twenty-seven years slipped away before someone else made the same trip. We are incredibly fortunate to have world-class wilderness in our backyard to explore.

Opposite: John swims in the "perfect tarn" perched high on a ridge above the junction of the Clear and Kingcome Rivers. *LB*

Lisa Baile gazes out over sunken lakes on the Powell Divide. *JB*

CHAPTER THREE:

WHALES AND ICEFIELDS

To be bound to one slope, even to one mountain, by a lift may be convenient but it robs us of the greatest pleasure that skiing can give, that is, to travel through the wide, wintry country; to follow the lure of the peaks which tempt on the horizon and to be alone for a few days or even a few hours in clear, mysterious surroundings.

—Hans Gmoser

Icefields adorn the Coast Mountains like a string of pearls laid along the spine of the range, in some places drowning all but the highest summits. These icefields form the core of some of the largest remaining areas of wilderness left in North America. Every year in May, as the winter storms start to wind down with a shift to calmer spring weather, we head up into one of these remote, icy places. The trips are similar to our three-week ski traverse of the Homathko Icefield. Our usual objective is to traverse an icefield but the real goal is to spend time in wilderness regions. These trips combine our love of wilderness with our love of skiing.

Each year we visit a new icefield and over the years we have moved north into Alaska. The basic nature of the mountains remains the same as you move north: the mountains rise from the shores of the ocean and their peaks are draped in ice, but there is something different about skiing Alaska. It is a land of extremes, where the glaciers come down to sea level, and stretches of bad weather can last for weeks. Our experience of this fairy-tale land of rugged granite spires and huge expanses of ice can be seen in the accounts of two of our trips: to the glaciers and peaks surrounding Glacier Bay and the Juneau Icefield.

Glacier Bay Traverse

A virtuous man, when alone, loves the quiet of the mountains. A wise man in nature enjoys the purity of the water. One must not be suspicious of the fool who takes pleasure in mountains and streams, but rather measure how well he sharpens his spirit by them.
—Muso Soseki, fourteenth-century Buddhist monk

Spring ski traverses on the coast are intimately connected with the ocean. Nowhere has this connection been stronger than on our traverse across the head of Glacier Bay. In April 2003, together with Gord Ferguson, Vince Mantle, Stan Sovdat and Lars Wilke, we set off from the shores of Chilkat Inlet, walking along gravel beaches while snowy peaks glistened in the sunshine. We turned up the valley south of Sullivan Mountain and climbed up onto the first of many glaciers on our second day. For the rest of the trip, though we travelled across massive glaciers, we were never more than 35 km from salt water and could see the ocean on most days.

Above: A small skier descends to the Grand Pacific Glacier. Our route continued up the long arm of the glacier visible in the background. *JB*

Left: The first day of our three-week ski trip across the mountains at the head of Glacier Bay began with a walk along the shore of Chilkat Inlet. *JB*

Lars Wilke and Stan Sovdat cross the Casement Glacier in Glacier Bay National Park. Glacier Bay is visible in the distance. On most days of our trip we could see the ocean from up high on the glaciers. *JB*

Our plan was to ski across the icefields at the head of Glacier Bay from Chilkat Inlet, south of Haines, to Dry Bay on the Gulf of Alaska and climb Mount Fairweather at the end of our trip if the weather cooperated. We had placed two food caches by ski plane. The pilot had warned us about the terrible conditions this year and recommended that we cancel our trip because snowpack levels were one third of normal and the glaciers were so full of crevasses that he thought we would never get through. After some deliberation we reasoned that since these icefields get more snow in one year than some ski areas get in ten years, there would still be quite a bit of snow around, so we decided to go for it.

We picked up our first food cache on our third day, at the head of the south branch of the Casement Glacier. We had come to respect every drop of sunshine in this part of the world, so after the first few sunny days we began to wonder if we were due for a big storm. The good weather kept holding as we continued west through the Takhinsha Mountains. The boggies we towed were perfect for the terrain, sliding easily as we crossed the various branches of the huge glaciers flowing into Glacier Bay. We climbed through a gorgeous pass beside Sitth-gha-ee Peak, to be greeted with views of sky-high Mount Fairweather looming in the distance. A carefree descending glide took us down to a camp on the McBride Glacier. Here, a wide band of enormous crevasses blocked the entrance to the west branch of the glacier. We roped up and were able to find a relatively easy route through the centre of the glacier. At lunch we saw

Evening view from camp up a side valley south of the Grand Pacific Glacier. *LB*

goats feeding on slopes above the glacier and wondered how much easier these trips would be if we didn't have to bring along so much food. Late in the afternoon we dropped our heavy loads and skied up a gentle snow dome west of Black Mountain. From the summit we could see numerous glaciers cascading down into Glacier Bay. It was remarkable to see how close to the ocean we were.

LINDA'S JOURNAL: Being here on the Grand Pacific Glacier reminds me of a kayak trip I did to Glacier Bay many years ago. I was impressed by the icy summits and massive glaciers but never imagined I would one day be skiing amongst them. Yet skiing up these huge glaciers now is somehow strangely similar to the feel of kayaking up the inlets that lie below.

This was the hottest day of the trip, with no wind, so that night we didn't bother to build our usual protective snow wall around the tent. The next morning we were caught completely off guard by strong gusts of wind that were trying to flatten our tents. At one point during the worst of the gusts, while Vince happened to be outside putting on his boots, a sudden blast of wind pushed the tent walls against us, nearly breaking the tent poles. We pressed our backs against the tent walls to hold the tent up from the inside as best we could. Curious as to how Vince was managing, we asked him what it was like outside, and in his typical reserved British style he replied,

Opposite, clockwise from top left: Aerial view of the Fairweather Range on the west side of Glacier Bay. *JB*

Close-up view of building-sized crevasses on the Grand Plateau Glacier. *LB*

Linda walks along the shore of Alsek Lake, with ice cliffs at the snout of the Grand Plateau Glacier in the background. This photo shows the extent of glacial recession in the area—less than forty years earlier the entire scene was buried under ice. *JB*

"It's a bit windy." The wind lasted for the rest of the day as we moved out onto the Riggs Glacier, keeping things much cooler than the previous day and making for a very icy side trip to an unnamed peak.

Beyond the Riggs, we had to down climb a steep snow slope to get onto the Muir Glacier. The weather continued clear as we skirted the vast emptiness of the Tsirku Icefield and traversed through a group of unnamed peaks onto the Carroll Glacier over the following few days. The scenery southwest of the Carroll Glacier was spectacular, and we spent another hot day crossing the divide onto the Tenas Tikke Glacier. The top of the Tenas Tikke Glacier was badly crevassed and we had to wind our way through some gaping slots in the ice. While crossing a narrow snow bridge between two crevasses, Stan cut the corner too sharply and his crazy carpet full of supplies slipped over the edge and dangled in the dark abyss. Luckily, Gord came to the rescue and was able to pull the crazy carpet out of the hole. Once clear of the crevasses, we revelled in the long, gentle coast down the Tenas Tikke Glacier, in awe of the enormous Grand Pacific Glacier we were approaching. Compared to many other mountainous regions of the world, elevation seemed to be a meaningless measure of the terrain: though we camped a mere 10 km from Tarr Inlet at only 600 m above sea level, the glacier was still over 6 km wide and we were opposite a huge jumble of seracs and crevasses, with the spectacular peaks of the Fairweather Range towering beyond us to the west.

We were a bit slow the next morning, as we had not had any rest in over ten days, so when we reached a nunatak in the middle of the glacier after lunch, we did not get moving again. This was a stunning spot to camp, with sweeping views down to Tarr Inlet and Glacier Bay, and we saw several icebergs calve off the Margerie Glacier into the sea. It was satisfying to camp on land (albeit snow-covered) instead of on a glacier.

We spent the next several days skiing up the Grand Pacific Glacier to our second airdrop, at the 1,400 m pass leading west onto the Grand Plateau Glacier. It was a rare treat to wash socks in some blue melt pools on the surface of the glacier. The highlight here was a side trip we made up the glacier west of Mount Eliza, which was a narrow ribbon of snow walled in by 1,500 m faces on all sides.

Beyond our airdrop we descended towards the Grand Plateau Glacier. Here the warnings of the ski plane pilot began to ring true and the lack of snow really did make things difficult. Below 1,200 m we roped up and at about 900 m we ran into a constriction where the glacier squeezed between sheer rock walls and gaping crevasses stretched across its entire width. Feeling completely blocked, we dropped our packs and skied up a peak on the side of the glacier to get a better view of our route.

From the summit the entire Grand Plateau Glacier came into view, dropping over 4,600 m into the Gulf of Alaska right from the summit of Mount Fairweather. Having been lucky with two weeks of sunshine, we had arrived early at this point, with extra food, and still entertained the idea of climbing Mount Fairweather. What we saw before us now was sobering. The entire glacier below 800 m was bare ice broken into

Pages 60–61: We made a side trip up this stunning steep-walled valley on the south side of the Grand Pacific Glacier. *LB*

a maze of crevasses that stretched for over 20 km to Alsek Lake. As we gazed west in the soft evening light, it became apparent that just getting out was going to be a real adventure.

The next morning, we awoke to fog and wet snowflakes and knew that our luck with the weather was over. At least this was more like the Alaska we had expected. From our vantage point above the glacier, Gord determined that we could probably get through the constriction of crevasses blocking the glacier by climbing through the seracs below camp. We roped up and started post-holing through the wet snow up and over the jumble of ice ridges. Eventually we made it past the constriction and were able to ski again. It didn't last long, though, because we started to run out of snow. Soaking wet, we set up camp on the last thin patch of snow on the bare ice and shivered in our wet clothes while we ate dinner. We slept in the next morning and rested the entire day—our first rest day in two weeks. It snowed and rained all day. We still had five days' food left, but as we continued down the glacier in rain and wet snow the next day, we realized that we might need every bit of it. We skied a little further on a mixture of wet slush and bare ice, then bypassed another major crevassed section by climbing through mud and rocks on the side of the glacier before swinging north towards Alsek Lake. Here we switched to crampons and wandered for hours through mazes of crevasses, eventually setting up camp on a small flat area of bare ice between two large crevasses.

Our camp on the ice in the never-ending sea of crevasses on the lower reaches of the Grand Plateau Glacier. We are heading to Alsek Lake, just visible in the background. *LB*

Above: The sandy shores on the Gulf of Alaska at the end of our trip. *JB*

Left: Gord Ferguson watches the morning light play on icebergs floating in Alsek Lake. *LB*

The next day the madness continued. Most of our time was spent going back and forth around crevasses, making very little progress down the glacier. Lars declared that he felt like a rat in a maze. By afternoon we realized that we had to get out of it. Eventually we found a way to the edge of the glacier and continued cramponing through a contorted landscape of huge piles of sand and rubble over jumbled ice left by the receding glacier. The following morning we walked under a large archway melted out of the stagnant ice on the side of the glacier. At the end of the day, we reached the beautiful shores of Alsek Lake, where we all sprawled around a campfire. The weather had started to improve slightly and the odd burst of sunshine lit up icebergs floating in the lake.

One more day of clambering along the boulder-strewn lakeshore took us to the start of a rough ATV track to the remote gravel airstrip at Dry Bay. Before catching our flight back to Haines Junction we made the 12 km return trip out to the beach at Dry Bay. In our clunky ski boots, we almost gave up in the endless sand dunes and grass that extended back from the beach for several kilometres, but it was worth every step when we reached the ocean. Soft sand swooped down to the pounding surf, and the afternoon sun shone on the glassy sea as we stared out into the Gulf of Alaska. The beach stretched as far as we could see, and towering in the distance among the clouds were the shimmering white peaks of the Fairweather Range.

I managed a quick rinse in the icy water while Stan found a rare glass fishing ball that had travelled all the way from Japan. It was hard to imagine a more fitting end to a ski trip so intimately connected with the sea. Perhaps the highlight was when Linda spotted a humpback whale offshore. After all, how often do you see a whale on a ski trip?

Juneau Icefield

There are only two ways to live your life. One is as though nothing is a miracle. The other is as though everything is a miracle.
—Albert Einstein

When you were a kid growing up, you didn't really think trees grew. Of course you were told they did but when you looked at them each year they didn't look any different. Glaciers are a bit like trees: when you first start looking at them they seem the same every year. But over time we've learned that trees do grow, and glaciers are shrinking.

"Sunshine forecast for after the weekend" read the front-page headline. We were hunkered down in Juneau waiting out a storm that had dropped 13 cm of rain in the last five days. Even the ravens were seeking shelter under roof overhangs, with their wet feathers sticking out at odd angles. Coming from the south coast we are used to rain, but the north coast takes it up a notch. Waiting for the weather to improve before starting our three-week ski trip, we checked the NOAA forecasts regularly and were amused by whole paragraphs full of terminology about the expected types of rain. The best was "heavy showers embedded in steady rain."

Linda carries skis up the Blackerby Ridge trail to reach the Juneau Icefield. The trail to the icefield starts on a residential street in Juneau less than 100 m from the ocean. *JB*

We had been waiting for a break in the weather and this was it. We made our final preparations and on May 5, 2014, started our ski traverse of the Juneau Icefield along with Diana Diaconu and Gord Ferguson. Juneau is one of the only cities in North America to have an icefield out its back door. We got a taxi ride to Wire Street where, less than 100 m from the ocean, a rough trail starts between several houses and heads into the forest. The trail climbed steeply onto Blackerby Ridge and within an hour or so we were skiing. Up into the mist and fog we went. The storm was a little slower at clearing than expected, so we camped under some ancient-looking mountain hemlocks draped with lichen.

The following morning we awoke to a glorious day and continued along the ridge, scattering flocks of ptarmigan that seemed to be revelling in the sunshine as well. We kicked steps up the last steep rise in the ridge to Cairn Peak, looking down at the ocean below. Everything in Alaska is extreme, from the weather to the scenery. Sitting in the warm evening sun, we soaked up the tremendous views of the distant white peaks of the Chilkat Range glistening above Lynn Canal, and a maze of islands stretching out to the Gulf of Alaska. These are not quaint little islands, though; these are Alaskan islands complete with their own mountain ranges. One of the largest islands, Admiralty, has a population of 1,600—not people but grizzly bears.

Above: Blackerby Ridge is home to a large flock of ptarmigan. *JB*

Below: Diana Diaconu ascends the final slopes of Cairn Peak, high above the shores of Lynn Canal. Mount Fairweather is just visible in the distance on the top right. *JB*

Above: Sunset from our camp near Cairn Peak. The Pacific Ocean is just visible in the distance. *LB*

Right: The stunning expanse of ice at the head of the Mendenhall Glacier between Rhino Peak and the Taku Range. *JB*

Pages 66–67: Crossing deep rain runnels in the snow while descending to the Norris Glacier. *LB*

Our patience paid off and the weather kept holding. We crammed seventeen days of food and supplies into our toboggans and slowly worked our way onto the Juneau Icefield. At our low point on the Lemon Glacier, our GPS told us that the glacier had lost 150 m of ice since the 1960s—another shocking reminder that humankind's effects even reach into a place like this.

From Nugget Mountain we got our first glimpse of the gigantic glaciers that make up the Juneau Icefield. The scale and size of the place was hard to comprehend. With the good weather we put some kilometres on and camped near Mendenhall Towers with views of sharp black spires rising out of the icefield.

Spending a few days in this area exploring the peaks and spires was one of the main objectives of our trip, so it was heartbreaking to watch the clouds roll in after dinner. The barometer plummeted and a storm pinned us down with high winds and heavy snowfall. For the next four and a half days our world shrank to an area 10 m in diameter. The snow walls around our tent grew to a height of 2 m. The weather seemed to scream out to us, "Welcome to Alaska." And made it clear why the glaciers are so big. At first we appreciated the luxury of a rest, but there are limits to how much rest you need. Such storms, though not totally fun, force you to slow down and accept the glaciated landscape on its own terms.

We had to shovel out our tent several times a day during a five-day snowstorm at the head of the Mendenhall Glacier. *LB*

John crosses the Taku Glacier, with the stunning spire of The Tusk rising out of the icefield in the background. *LB*

On the afternoon of the fifth day the wind finally shifted to the west, signalling the storm would end soon, so we headed off into the swirling mist, using a compass and GPS to navigate. As we wandered into the endless white void, distant peaks started to emerge from the mist and we were treated to primordial views of the stunning spires of Rhino Peak, Taku Towers and Horn Spire jutting out of the pancake-flat icefield.

After a very cold night we turned the corner onto the main branch of the Taku Glacier. Our route took us across three lobes of the glacier. At this point the glacier was a whopping 15 km wide and virtually flat. For the entire afternoon we skied in a straight line, hour after hour, with the peaks crawling past us, absorbing the power exuded by the enormous expanse of ice and awed by the realization that all of it was shifting, moving and flowing slowly towards a big ice cliff by the ocean some 50 km away.

Clouds boiling up from the surrounding valleys and lenticular clouds forming on the peaks on the north side of the icefield told us that another storm was coming, so we pushed on for several more hours to a tiny glaciology hut perched high up on a ridge on the far side of the icefield. Our extra effort was worth it—fierce winds and snow blasted the hut for two days. Despite being walled in by a wind cirque, the tiny hut was palatial compared to our tents. The cabin was constructed in the 1960s and is one of several built by glaciologists who have been studying the surrounding glaciers since 1946. Buried under one of the plywood bunks we found a 1968 REI catalogue,

which provided hours of entertainment. The changes in outdoor gear over forty-six years were amazing to us, but to the glaciers outside, forty-six years was a mere ripple in their history. Yet the glaciologists' notes in the hut logbook described how the icefield was wasting away at all elevations. It is staggering to see the speed at which climate change is affecting something as massive as this icefield. The latest forecasts predict that 70 percent of the glaciers in western Canada could be gone by 2100.

A stiff north wind blew the storm away but created a ground blizzard that we had to ski directly into. With scarves covering our faces we headed north across the border into Canada and onto the Llewellyn Glacier, the crest of the icefield. Where the Taku was simply enormous, the Llewellyn in comparison felt like a cross between the Prairies and the moon.

We considered making a side trip to one of the peaks ringing the horizon but the closest one was more than 10 km away so we decided to keep moving north across the Llewellyn Glacier. When it became clear we were heading down and off the icefield, Diana summed up everybody's feelings when she said, "Goodbye, icefield." We were grieving the fact that we hadn't been able to do many side trips, but also realized that the searing beauty of the icefield had sunk deep into our bones. It was hard to leave.

Lower down, Atlin Lake came into view in the distance. The lake was ice-free and we hoped that our original plan to canoe back to the town of Atlin would be possible,

Top: Seracs at the snout of the Llewellyn Glacier tower behind John. *LB*

Above: Linda compares her footprint to that of a resident grizzly bear. *LB*

but after a quick call on our sat phone we found out the lake was still frozen at the other end. Soon after that we skied to the toe of the glacier and climbed down off the ice to camp on a gravel bar beside a meltwater stream coming off the glacier. In the morning we strapped our skis to our packs and continued down onto textured outwash gravel flats. Having just come off the frozen icefield, seeing running water, gravel bars and dry grass was a shock. It was like walking from winter to spring in one day. We passed three lakes on our way. The biggest was chock full of icebergs and was so stunningly beautiful that we decided to camp early. We spent the afternoon watching the play of light on the seracs and icebergs from the Llewellyn Glacier. A grizzly walked by camp, and later we saw a porcupine.

The recession of the Llewellyn Glacier has had dramatic effects on the surrounding landscape. Our map showed that in the 1970s the lake we were camped beside was still buried under the glacier terminus. As the glacier receded it formed two lakes on either side of a headland, one draining north into Llewellyn Inlet, and the other draining northeast into Sloko Inlet. In 2011 continued recession of the glacier allowed water from the upper lake to burst through the ice and connect the two lakes, causing

Above: View of the morning light on the snout of the Llewellyn Glacier. This spot was so spectacular that we camped early the day before so that we would have more time here. *JB*

Right: Early morning view of Atlin Lake at sunrise. *LB*

a huge flood down one of the valleys and forever lowering the level of the first lake so that the river draining it became dry.

On our last day of travel we left behind the iceberg-filled lake and travelled down the recently dried-up riverbed to Atlin Lake, with a curious goat paralleling us on high cliffs. At Atlin Lake we were greeted by the echoing call of a pair of loons. We camped on a smooth sandy beach right next to the reflection of the snowy peaks in the glassy calm water. The silence and stillness of this wild place left a feeling of deep peace inside us. We relaxed in the hauntingly beautiful location for a full day before taking a short helicopter flight to Atlin.

The weather in Alaska can be unpredictable, from the exceptionally dry weather in 2003 to the wet stormy spring in 2013, but the question we ask ourselves is, in a land already known for extremes, are the extremes becoming more severe, as climate change predicts? It's hard to tell from year to year but when we look back over many years we see that the tree in our backyard is growing and the glaciers all across North America are receding. It feels like we are watching these magnificent glaciers and icefields shrink and disappear forever.

Linda, Diana and Gord take their first few steps on bare ground after climbing off the snout of the Llewellyn Glacier. *JB*

CHAPTER FOUR

GENTLE WILDERNESS

And forget not that the earth delights to feel your bare feet
and the winds long to play with your hair.

—Kahlil Gibran

Almost at treeline, we were in a dense stretch of willow, climbing up a broad gully onto the Dil-Dil Plateau, when all of a sudden we saw a grizzly bear rise up on her hind legs, making woofing sounds and clicking her jaw. We quickly backed out of the willow, while the mother grizzly gathered her cubs and moved swiftly across the slope away from us. With an extra shot of adrenalin, we scurried in the opposite direction from the bear and continued up the slope.

We are always thrilled to see these wonderful animals. They are magnificent—truly impressive in size and strength. Fear is a natural reaction of ours, of course, and encounters with bears force us to be humble. They can be aggressive and are easily capable of killing a person, but it is an extremely rare occurrence, and we have never had a bad encounter with a bear.

Grizzly bears are intelligent, curious animals that are mostly reclusive and live primarily off plants, seeds, roots, insects and salmon. Their long claws are specially

adapted for digging. Grizzlies are often called a keystone species, as their presence is an indicator of the overall health of a wilderness region.

British Columbia is one of the last strongholds for grizzly bears in Canada. They require large areas of wilderness for their habitat and live primarily in the remaining rugged mountain wilderness. One female will range over several large alpine valleys and males can cover an area twice that size. Finding this kind of intact wilderness is getting harder in southwestern BC. Though there is still a significant amount of wilderness, the region is becoming more and more fragmented. Highways and small settlements in the main valleys have carved the region up into isolated pockets. Logging roads reaching to near treeline have decimated almost every valley. The remaining wilderness is high in the mountains. Some populations of bears, for example in the Stein River valley, have become cut off and isolated from other bear populations to the point where they are now genetically distinct. Add to this their very low reproductive rates and it is easy to see that the threats to this amazing animal are very real.

Morning light casts a gentle glow on peaks reflected in a serene lake in the South Chilcotin Mountains. *JB*

Above: Rhiannon Johnson crosses the upper reaches of Grant Creek in the South Chilcotin Mountains. *JB*

Right: Water droplets are displayed like jewels in the leaves of a lupine after a rainstorm. *JB*

In southwestern BC there are fewer than 300 grizzly bears between the US border and the Chilcotin Plateau, and grizzly bears are listed as threatened. The chance of seeing a grizzly bear is getting rarer and rarer. In comparison, the four contiguous national parks in the Rocky Mountains contain about 200 grizzlies and over the border in Washington state's North Cascades National Park it appears there are no remaining grizzly bears. It is crucial that grizzly habitat in southwestern BC is not taken for granted.

After our encounter with the bear we climbed up onto the Dil-Dil Plateau and headed west across the tundra-like landscape towards Mount Vic. We were on an eight-day hike in the Chilcotin Ranges in southwestern BC. As you move east into the rain shadow of the Coast Mountains the ranges become drier and the heavy glaciation thins out to leave extensive alpine meadows in place of the vast icefields. The Chilcotin Ranges are the last mountains before the Chilcotin Plateau, and a gentle wilderness where swaths of meadows and flowers carpet the hillsides, stands of aspen line grassy clearings in the forest, and broad passes and rambling ridges connect the summits.

We camped on the shores of Vic Lake in the high alpine and scrambled up the steep rocky slopes of Mount Vic to one of the last high summits before the edge of the Chilcotin Plateau. In one direction we could see out over that vast plateau. In the other we looked back to a sea of mountains stacked up against the horizon. Spread out below us was the wide expanse of the Dil-Dil Plateau, which we had crossed.

We were in the midst of Big Creek Provincial Park and the adjoining South Chilcotin Mountains Provincial Park, created in 1995 and 2010 respectively. Together they make up a vast territory of world-class parkland. The landscape is dominated by gently sloping valleys and dome-shaped summits, and features everything from alpine meadows to fossils and lava beds. It provides especially rich and diverse habitats for a variety of wildlife including grizzly bears, black bears, wolves, deer, moose, mountain goats, bighorn sheep and wolverines.

The parks fall within the territory of the Tsilhqot'in, St'át'imcets and Secwepemc First Nations. Travelling by horse and on foot, they established many routes that now form a network of trails criss-crossing the region. Today the trails are travelled exten-

Linda was taking a photo of these flowers just as a hummingbird happened to fly into the camera frame. It was only when she got home and looked at the photo carefully that she realized she had actually captured two hummingbirds. *LB*

sively on foot, by horse and by mountain bike, making this a wilderness recreational paradise. Any number of loops and trips can be done.

Everywhere, the rich natural history is part of a complex and interconnected web of life that is spread across the region. We see mule deer that migrate to the high grasslands for their summer range from as far as the Fraser River. At treeline there is always the distinct cry of the Clark's nutcracker. This unique bird is characteristic of the area and is known for its interdependent relationship with the whitebark pine, a tall bushy tree that favours the drier soil near treeline. The seeds of the whitebark pine are wingless, so they cannot be carried any distance by the wind. Instead, seed dispersal is carried out by Clark's nutcrackers, who harvest their preferred food with their long, pointed, sturdy bills and store a few seeds at a time in numerous underground caches. Red squirrels also feed heavily on whitebark pine seeds and cache the pine cones in large middens. These middens are in turn raided by grizzly bears and serve as an important, high-nutrient food source for them. Grizzly bear foraging is also visible in the alpine meadows, where we routinely come across overturned earth where bears have been digging for the bulbs of avalanche lilies and feeding on cow parsnip, horsetails and dandelion.

Wildlife is one of the highlights of these summer trips. In contrast to the austere world of the icefields we ski across in the spring, these vibrant alpine meadows are teeming with life. Marmots are everywhere. As we walk through the alpine we are accompanied by a travelling wave of whistles warning other marmots of our presence. But the larger, more elusive animals, like the grizzly, are the ones we find it such a privilege to see. During one summer trip, while pausing to rest on an alpine slope, we were startled by the barking of a wolf on a ridge high above us. We saw the wolf and his family several times over the next few days, watching the pups run through alpine meadows and listening to their howls echoing from the walls of the surrounding peaks. It was a brief glimpse into their world. We wondered, what do the mountains look like through their eyes? What guides them across the landscape? It was fascinating to imagine, even for a brief moment, a different perspective—one completely removed from our own human-centred view.

One of our oddest wildlife sightings was of a large black shape ascending a small glacier to cross a high pass. We watched the figure move up the ice and it took us a while to realize what it was. Only when the large animal turned sideways on the ridge crest did we recognize the profile. It was a moose and her calf. Moose love lowlands and swampy areas, so we were completely surprised to see one high in the alpine, especially with a calf. Perhaps the most disconcerting thing we have seen involved a goat. As we climbed over a ridge and started down the other side we spotted a nanny goat and her kid on a patch of snow below. Goats are normally pretty wary but these two looked particularly agitated. Looking through binoculars we could just make out the legs of an unborn kid dangling from the nanny. No wonder she was distressed. We wondered how long she had been in this predicament and fantasized about catching her and helping somehow. But of course as soon as we started towards her she ran off.

Top: A bee investigates a pink monkey flower. *JB*

Above: As John crossed a high alpine meadow he almost stepped on these young birds in a ground nest. *JB*

Opposite: John passes a small tarn in the upper reaches of Slim Creek in the South Chilcotin Mountains. *LB*

Pages 82–83: Expansive alpine meadows in the South Chilcotin Mountains. *JB*

Above: Indian paintbrush. *JB*

Right: Linda wades through a fiery patch of Indian paintbrush in the South Chilcotin Mountains. *JB*

A panoramic view of the lush green slopes of McGillivray Pass. *JB*

The powerful storms and heavy snows of winter are what characterize the climate of the Coast Mountains. But in a sense, winter is also what defines how splendid the summers are. The contrast between the deep winter snow and the alpine wildflowers is truly breathtaking. We are always amazed at how we can be skiing in May and then just a few weeks later we can be wading through vibrant fields of alpine flowers. The transformation of a brown and lifeless hillside that is buried under snow for

eight months into a lush garden of knee-deep flowers is one of the most astounding feats of nature. Nowhere is the cycle of life over the seasons so dazzling as in the alpine, where winters and summers are accentuated by the higher elevation.

Summer is a time to wander and revel in the beauty and diversity of alpine meadows—the gentle wilderness that contrasts so sharply with the glaciers of the rugged peaks near the spine of the Coast Mountains. In addition to the Chilcotin Ranges, our summer trips have taken us to many of the alpine areas up and down the east side of the range. The closest trips to our home in Vancouver are to the mountains of southwestern BC. Squeezed between the deep valleys of the Squamish, Lillooet, Bridge and Stein Rivers, the intervening systems of ridges, alpine valleys and summits form isolated mountain ranges that offer blocks of wilderness. We have been exploring these areas one by one, reaching deep into the heart of each region on week-long trips spent roaming across the landscape, scrambling over rugged ridge tops, wading across rainbow-coloured hillsides of wildflowers and camping by crystal-clear lakes.

Over the years, the trips and our experiences blend together in our memories. The sprawling blur of steep meadows, vibrant flowers and stunning lakes nestled among the high rocky peaks of the Cadwallader Range merges with the jagged range of mountains that rims the deep rectangular drainage of the Stein River, and these in turn join with the narrow uplifts of green ridge tops towering above surrounding valleys in the Cayoosh Range. And together they become part of our consciousness, pieced together like a collage to form an exquisite work of art more perfect than a Japanese garden.

A marmot watches us pass from a perch next to his den in the ground nearby. *JB*

CHAPTER FIVE:

SKI WILD

Feel the mountain and let it show you how you're going to ski it.

Relax and cruise. This isn't a fight, it's a dance, and the mountain

always leads.

—Jim Bowden

....

Pages 86–87: John looks west from Mount Cain across a sea of clouds to the Haihte Range on Vancouver Island. *LB*

Opposite: Dan Carey skis through a snow-covered rock field in soft mid-winter light. *JB*

Below: Mike Blenkarn weaves through the long shadow of a mountain peak. *JB*

The wind pressed our jackets firmly against our chests. It was the kind of wind you could lean your full body weight into. We stood on the middle summit of Mount Seymour as powerful gusts behind a clearing storm blasted the alpine areas. Over on the main summit, the wind swept up the steep southwest side of the mountain, creating strong updraft. More than forty ravens had gathered to soar on it. They would fold their wings and chase each other, diving and rolling in hot pursuit while making noises that sounded like pebbles being dropped into a pool of water. At the end of each plunge the ravens would catch the updraft and instantly rise several hundred metres to repeat the diving and tucking all over again.

Pages 90–91: Brad Zeerip rips down a 1500 m run from Alder Peak in the Kitimat Ranges. *LB*

Below: Strong backlighting illuminates the snow spray from Brad Zeerip's skis. *JB*

Bottom: Chris McCrum hot-dogging. *LB*

Maybe Hans Gmoser had also been watching ravens when he said, "A man should have wings to carry him where his dreams go but sometimes a pair of skis make a good substitute." For us, backcountry skiing is the closest we will ever get to being ravens. Using touring bindings that allow us to walk on our skis and "skins" for grip, we roam the high ridges and peaks like the ravens, free to wander and ski where our hearts lead us and to roll with the spirit of the earth.

In winter, storms roll in off the North Pacific Ocean and wash the western edge of British Columbia with waves of moisture like the barnacles endure in the surf below. This constant lashing plasters whipped-cream dollops of snow on the peaks and smears it across the ridges and bowls.

What is it about snow? What is it that draws kids to make snow angels, or run their hands and feet through the snow? And what is it about making ski tracks through fresh powder that draws out the child in all of us?

In winter, skiing is our life. It is part of our seasonal migration from green to white, from sweeping hillsides of alpine flowers to snow-plastered trees and snowflakes dancing in the air. We start our trips with a slow, steady climb up through a wintery

forest, with snow settled in deep under the trees. All sounds are muffled by the blanket of snow, and the old-growth forest stands in total silence, as it has for hundreds of years. The cool air on our cheeks is invigorating. The steady rhythm of climbing uphill is meditative and produces an inner quiet. We are suspended above the ground by the snow. The landscape takes over and imparts a sense of flow as we move slowly up the hill, curving around the side of the mountain and wrapping it with our winding ski track. Up we climb, eager for the descent, but also basking in the peace and solitude of the ascent. Winter is a time to look inward—a time to enrich the soul.

As we wind our way to the top of our run, the air is often thick with snowflakes. We remove our skins and the anticipation builds as we switch our bindings to downhill mode. With a push over the edge we are off, curving and swooping our way down the mountainside with snow spraying in the air. Feeling the soft snow under our skis we play with it, carving and sculpting as we steer through this mouldable medium. When the snow is deep, it sprays onto our chests and flies in our faces, and only our speed enables us to float on top, suspended on the frozen crystals.

It is exhilarating to lay down the first set of ski tracks in a vast wilderness, as if

Following pages: The tranquility of a winter wonderland. *LB*

Above: Branches of whitebark pine reach out to collect puffy balls of freshly fallen snow. *LB*

Left: John engulfed in champagne powder as he descends to the Asulkan valley. *LB*

Ross Mailloux creates an impressive plume of cold smoke in Cerise Creek. *JB*

painting on an empty white canvas. Our tracks are an expression of joy written on a temporary canvas that will soon be washed clean with the next snowfall. But back-country skiing is not just about the exciting downhill—it is also about the tranquility of moving gracefully through the mountain wilderness. Our skis become the tools we use to interact with the winter landscape. They allow us to revel in the spirit of winter, to swoop down from the summit of a high mountain peak or seek out the snowy winter glades of an old-growth forest, and to connect with the wilderness in a totally different manner than we are used to. In 1921 Sir Arnold Lunn described this well in his book *Alpine Skiing at All Heights and Seasons*, with the words: "There are many who find in the combination of skiing and mountaineering the finest of all sports, for whom no ski tour is perfect unless it includes the ascent of some big peak, or traverse of some great glacier pass, and also yields the ski-runner the unfettered joy of a perfect unhampered run down some great glacier. It is not merely skiing, it

is not merely scenery that draws us to the glaciers on skis. It is rather the knowledge that the skiing motion seems to lend a new significance to mountain beauty, so that the impressions gained in some run down a glacier highway are deeper, more vivid and more enduring than those which reward the man on foot."

Days blend together and there is a flow to the winter season. In the dead of winter the high peaks and icefields are shrouded in bad weather and our ski journeys stay closer to the treeline. Here we search for deep powder in glades and meadows. As the days grow longer and the weather improves, we will venture higher and higher into big alpine bowls and ski across vast glaciers. The tranquility of the glades will be replaced by the shimmering white of the alpine. But for now our souls get to play in the deep snow like the ravens soaring and rolling on the updraft.

Distant skiers silhouetted on a ridge below Metal Dome. *LB*

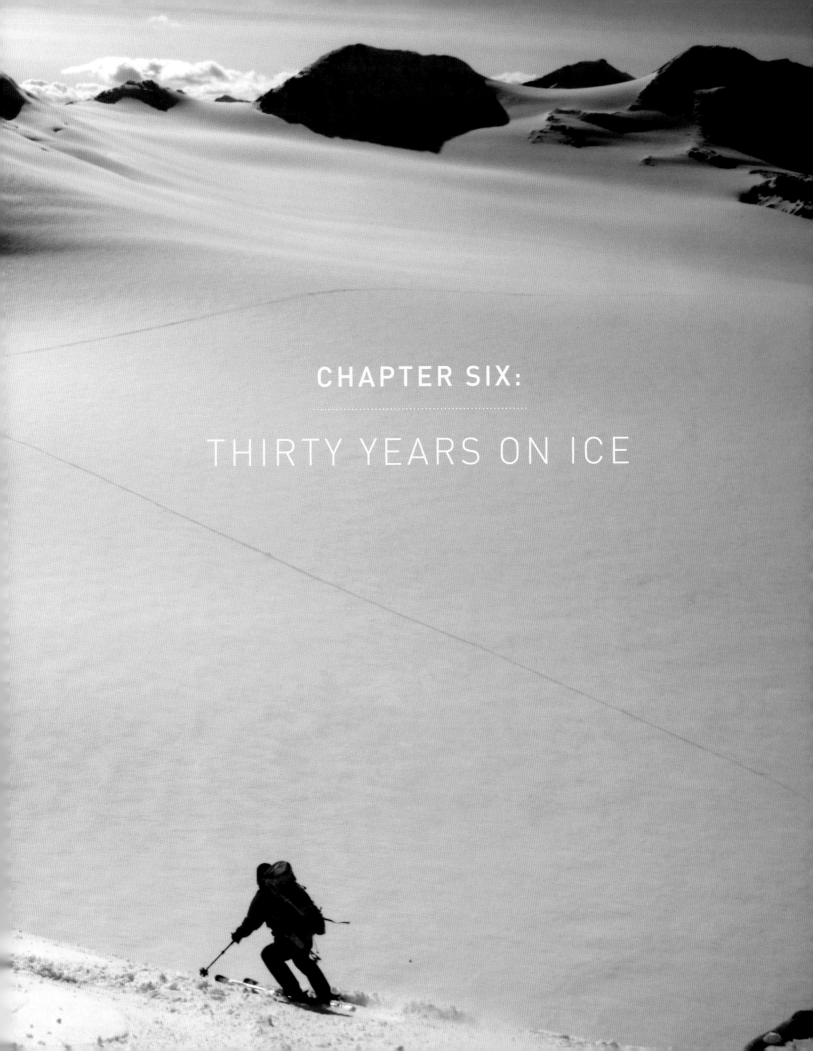

CHAPTER SIX:

THIRTY YEARS ON ICE

Range after range of mountains

Year after year after year.

I am still in love.

—Gary Snyder

Pages 98–99: Brian Hall skis off Mount Mills at the head of the Frank Smith Glacier. *JB*

Opposite: A skier passes under seracs on the Ring Glacier. *LB*

Below: Our trip across the Lillooet Icefield started on the shores of Lower Taseko Lake. *JB*

This chapter describes a ski trip across the Lillooet Icefield that we took in 2010, exactly thirty years after John first completed it with a group of friends in 1980. It first appeared as an article in the *Canadian Alpine Journal*.

We followed the footprints up the Tchaikazan River valley for several days. They belonged to a large grizzly and dwarfed those of my ski boots. The bear had sunk deep into the spring snow on the wide gravel flats beside the river. We crossed his tracks many times on our way up the wide, U-shaped valley, staring at the sharp rocky peaks that rise up to 1,400 m above the river.

Our trip had started from Taseko Lakes at the end of April 2010. After a boat ride across the Taseko River, it had taken us two days to follow an old mining road into the Tchaikazan River valley. Halfway up the valley we camped for two nights beside

Above: Panoramic view of the Tchaikazan River valley from near Spectrum Pass. *JB*

Opposite: A grizzly and her two cubs cross the lower part of the Tchaikazan Glacier. *LB*

a dilapidated plywood shack and made a side trip to a 2,700 m peak above Spectrum Pass. At treeline we got a stunning panoramic view of the entire Tchaikazan valley rising in a long smooth arc from its depths in the forest, across gravel bars and meadows, to the glaciers and jagged summits at its headwaters. Spectrum Pass was a wide alpine area and from the summit we could see glimpses of Chilko Lake in the distance, like a sliver of ocean through wisps of cloud.

The curve of the main valley led us past the sheer north face of Moose Mountain, and we passed the spot where I had landed in a ski plane in May 1980 to begin my first ski traverse of the Lillooet Icefield. At that time, though, there had been a few short ski traverses in the Coast Mountains, but no one had really thought of doing a three-week trip across one of the large icefields, so we had no idea what to expect. Back then, we were a group of friends in their twenties embarking on the ski adventure of a lifetime. Now, thirty years later, I was planning to repeat the same trip—this time joined by Linda and a group of friends: Brian Hall, Coby Hall, Katy Chambers, Anne-Marie Baribeau, Mark Grist, Francis St. Pierre and Gord Bose. A lot happens in thirty years, both for us and for glaciers, and an icefield gives a good perspective on that length of time. I have skied across a different icefield almost every spring since 1980. For me this trip was an opportunity to reflect on and celebrate thirty years of skiing on the big icefields of the Coast Mountains.

At the head of the valley, where the river emerged from under the snout of the glacier, we skied up onto the snow-covered ice. The glacier had receded over a kilo-

metre in the past thirty years. From a camp at the top of the glacier, we split into two groups, with one group scrambling up the south ridge of Mount Monmouth and the other skiing up Corner Peak for a fabulous ski run on corn snow. After resupplying from a food cache on the Chapman Glacier, we made the steep descent onto the Edmond Glacier, climbed past some towering blue seracs to the col east of Sovereign Peak and descended to a camp above the lower Frank Smith Glacier. We sat in the sun on a tiny patch of heather that had just melted out of the deep spring snowpack. We had seen more bear tracks at the head of the valley, and it was great to be deep in the wilderness. According to my map we had camped in exactly the same spot in 1980, but I only had recollections of poorer weather.

The next morning we skied up the Frank Smith Glacier with our crazy carpet toboggans in tow. In 1980 we had used leather boots and narrow telemark skis with

Linda descends towards the Frank Smith Glacier. *JB*

aluminum edges. They were really just glorified cross-country skis, and for grip we used wax. I remember stopping halfway up the glacier to use white gas to try to remove klister wax from our skis so we could continue climbing higher in the fresh snow. We had climbed through a whiteout to the crest of the icefield at 2,600 m and desperately set up camp as quickly as we could before our single-leather boots started to freeze. Now with warm plastic boots we leisurely set up camp in the sunshine before skiing up Mount Mills for a panoramic view of the flat expanse of ice that forms the headwaters of the Bridge and Stanley Smith Glaciers. This is something I will never tire of—the shimmering silence of an icefield. It is hard to imagine the enormous mass of snow and ice moving, but glaciers are like rivers. The patterns and shapes of the icefield were basically the same as they had been in 1980, but over thirty years the actual ice had moved a distance of 5 to 10 kilometres.

Our camp at the head of the Frank Smith Glacier. *JB*

Perched on the summit of Mount Mills, Linda enjoys the panoramic view of the Lillooet Icefield. *JB*

Looking at my map, which had routes from my previous trips marked on it, made me feel old. In 1980 we had also climbed Mount Mills, but it was one of six peaks that we had climbed in a single day. I guess we were doing well for our age, but we definitely didn't have the energy we had in our early twenties.

Day 10 saw us heading south across the icefield. We skied up the 2,900 m summit immediately southwest of Stanley Peak only to be surprised by a group of seven snowmobilers on top. We chatted for a while. They were all friendly guys from Pemberton and Whistler. But what a contrast: we were ten days into the wilderness; they were just out for a day trip. In 1980 it was guaranteed you wouldn't see anyone in a place like this. Only a few climbing parties had ever been to the Lillooet Icefield,

and we had most likely been the only ski party in the 500 km stretch of mountains between Pemberton and Bella Coola.

We had a great run southwest from Stanley Peak and camped at the crest of the Ring Glacier. We dug a comfortable kitchen and dined in the evening light. Brian and Coby posed for some father and son photos, and Brian made a sat phone call home and learned that his second grandchild had just been born.

The next morning we made two side trips. The climbing types headed west to use their ice axes while the skiers went for the corn on the south-facing slopes of Mount Alecto. When planning this trip, one of the things I hoped for most was to be able to ski these slopes in good conditions. In thirty years of exploring all those icefields,

Pages 108–109: John and Francis St. Pierre pick a ski route beneath towering seracs on the Edmond Glacier. *LB*

Above: Brian and Coby Hall head across the expansive upper Ring Glacier, with Mount Tisiphone behind. *JB*

Right: Linda looks south across the Ring Glacier from the summit of Stanley Peak. *JB*

few places stand out as offering a more scenic location for a spring ski run. The south slopes of Mount Alecto lie perched 1,000 m above the trench of the Lillooet Glacier with a backdrop of the 1,500 m north faces of Lillooet Mountain and Mount Tisiphone rising above the four-way junction of the Lillooet, Ring and Bishop Glaciers. The weather was absolutely perfect. After a straightforward ascent to the summit we were ready for our descent just as the snow started to soften in the midday sun. Six of us leap-frogged down the mountainside, carving great arcs in the silken snow with huge icefalls in the background.

Back at camp we picked up our packs and enjoyed the last of the corn snow coasting down the Ring Glacier. At the bottom I was surprised to see that the surface of the Ring Glacier had receded to the point where it no longer connected to the Bishop Glacier, and the Bishop Glacier had receded so far as to create an iceberg-filled lake. Climate change wasn't even on the radar in 1980, but by now it was evident in all the glaciers in western Canada.

We climbed to our second food cache at the toe of the east ridge of Mount Tisiphone. Perched above the seracs, this was a scenic spot to camp. We continued up the Lillooet Glacier in the morning and we could make out an old set of ski tracks that we later found out were made by a young couple on their honeymoon. While our

Brian and Coby Hall leapfrog down perfect corn snow on the south slopes of Mount Alecto, with Mount Tisiphone rising from the Lillooet Glacier behind. *JB*

111

Above: Gord Bose tows his crazy carpet tobaggan as we ascend to our second food cache. *LB*

Right: Coby Hall ascends Mount Alecto, with icefalls tumbling down Lillooet Mountain behind. *LB*

group had pioneered the route in 1980, it was now done annually. It was inspiring to see people out on the icefields, connecting with these wild and spectacular places.

From a camp on the plateau at 2,650 m, we skied up Mount Dalgleish. The ascent from the north side is straightforward as the snowfield butts right up against the peak. The surprise comes when you reach the summit and look down the other side at the Toba River, which lies in a 2,800 m deep trench walled in by steep mountains on both sides. Peering down the valley I could make out dozens of familiar peaks near the head of Toba Inlet. I had spent years in that country with John Clarke, and it brought back great memories. In 1980 I didn't know anything more than the major drainages and a few of the higher summits, but now in almost every direction I looked were familiar peaks. What once were only bumps on the horizon were now firmly etched in my soul. It wasn't just the accomplishments that were there; it was also the whole kaleidoscope of sights, sounds and feelings from years spent in the wilderness.

Seeing all these peaks was like looking back in time. A lot happens in three decades. Our original group of twenty-year-olds was now in their fifties. We had gone on with our lives. One of our group members was a math professor, three were mountain guides, another was a computer specialist and was now retired, and I had written three editions of a ski guidebook and produced several topographic maps.

Overlooking the shrinking Lillooet Glacier from a camp at our second food cache. *LB*

Children were born and grew up, and parents and siblings had died. Good times and tough times. But I was just as excited to see what lay ahead and to feel the wonders of this magical landscape as I felt thirty years ago.

The next morning, we down climbed a short, steep snow gully to get off the plateau and onto the long snowy spine that connects to the Manatee Range. This is a fabulous ski route that follows the crest of the ridge for 8 km. The ridge drops 1,500 m to deep valleys on either side, and there are awe-inspiring views in all directions, including the huge icefalls pouring off Mount Dalgleish and the Manatee Range. Pioneering the traverse in 1980, we were pinned down by bad weather and agonized whether to wait out the storm so we could travel the ridge, or take a low route. The group dynamics of making that decision were as challenging as the route-finding was for our energetic group of young skiers. Now older and mostly wiser, these sorts of issues had been replaced with other life challenges. Anne-Marie's partner, Hannes,

had died when he fell into a crevasse the previous year a mere 20 km to the west of where we were. Anne-Marie was still grieving, and travelling on a glacier was a struggle for her. We provided support as best we could, but as we got closer to the place where Hannes had died, it became too emotionally overwhelming and she decided to fly out. Using our sat phone, we called for a helicopter and an hour later Anne-Marie flew away, leaving us with that ringing silence that is left behind after a helicopter comes and goes.

Several days later Brian was feeling extremely tired and having a hard time taking a deep breath. Because of a known heart condition, Brian and his son Coby also made the choice to leave. After the trip, it was clear that both Brian and Anne-Marie had made the right decisions, but it is always hard at the time. In 1980 there were no sat phones, and no communication with the outside world was possible.

Springtime melt causes the creeks to swell thigh-deep. Mark Grist fords the chocolate waters of a branch of Meager Creek. *JB*

The pilot who came in to pick up Anne-Marie had said a big storm was moving in, so we made a push to travel the full length of the ridge and move to a camp at treeline in the Manatee Range. After two weeks on the go we were all beat, and several days of rain and wet snow provided a welcome rest.

Finally it cleared, and we headed off in two groups climbing Wahoo Tower and skiing up the west summit of Dugong Peak. The upper slopes offered our last powder skiing of the winter. Not bad for May 19.

Bad weather returned and forced us to abandon our planned high route out past Capricorn Mountain. Instead, we skied out to old logging roads on Meager Creek, crossing the thigh-deep muddy water in the afternoon. Rain, mist, bird songs and the smells of cottonwood and fir welcomed us to the valley. On our last day, we soaked in the hot springs before walking down the road to a pre-arranged pickup at the Lillooet River.

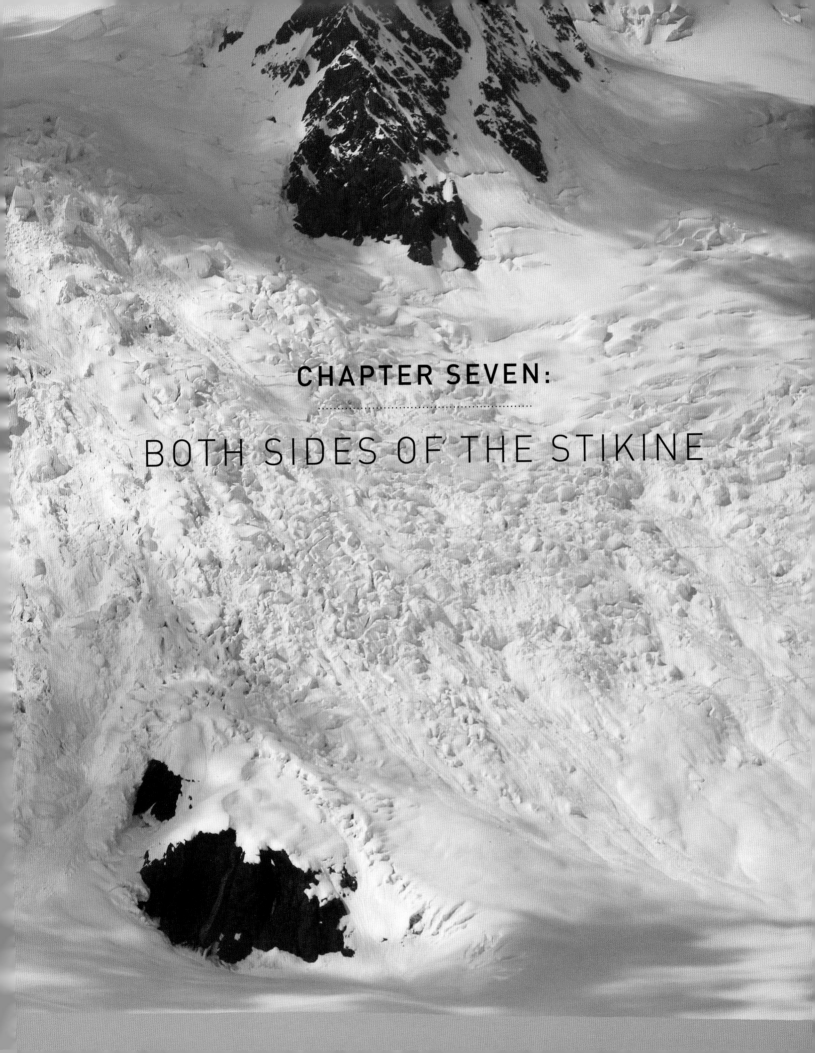

CHAPTER SEVEN:

BOTH SIDES OF THE STIKINE

Understand this about the Stikine: we are not just talking about a river. We are talking about one of the greatest stretches of running water on the planet.

—Mark Hume

J OHN'S JOURNAL: In the late 1970s, when it first occurred to me that you could ski across the big icefields of the Coast Mountains, I remember digging out dozens of maps and imagining all the trips that might be possible. The icefields of the Alaska Panhandle were the most obvious and the enormous icefield west of the Stikine River was so big it even stood out on a road map of BC. Straddling the border between Alaska and BC, the Stikine Icefield extends for over 190 km along the spine of the Coast Mountains and feeds the largest glaciers in the range, the longest of which are over 50 km long. At the time I was too busy exploring icefields in the southern Coast Mountains, but I remember reading with fascination about a 1984 ski traverse across the Stikine Icefield from the South Sawyer Glacier to the Great Glacier on the Stikine River. I also couldn't forget hearing about a similar trip the following year, where the skiers struggled through fifteen days of storm on a seventeen-day traverse.

So it was the fulfillment of a lifelong dream when in May 2002 two friends and I skied from Whiting Lake, at the north end of the icefield, to the Stikine River. This was a magnificent trip. The contrast between the big flat glaciers and the jagged peaks was absolutely stunning. After three weeks of wandering on the ice, we climbed the final ridge and were treated to a sweeping view of the green thread of the mighty Stikine River slicing through the ice-capped mountains. We finished on the banks of the river, and watched a huge grizzly bear swim across it while waiting for a jet boat from Wrangell to pick us up.

The memory of that spectacular mountain wilderness haunted me with a desire to return. Over the years I made several trips in the area but the highlights were two ski trips that Linda and I did, which contrasted the east and west sides of the Stikine River.

To the Iskut River

I thought of the wilderness we had left behind us, open to sea and sky, joyous in its plenitude and simplicity, perfect yet vulnerable, unaware of what is coming, defended by nothing, guarded by no one.
—Edward Abbey

The Coast Mountains are defined by water: the ocean and inlets, the mist and clouds, the rain and snow, the creeks and rivers, the glaciers and the icefields. All these

Loading our canoes and kayaks at Telegraph Creek before paddling down the Stikine River to the start of our three-week ski trip. *JB*

Above: We take advantage of a rare chance to refill our water bottles from this meltwater pool on an unnamed glacier near Mount Hickman. *JB*

Opposite right: John looks into an ice cave at the edge of an unnamed glacier south of the Scud River. *LB*

forms of water are continually moving over this land, moulding the character of the landscape. Nowhere on the coast is this more striking than in southeast Alaska. Over the last few years we have done a series of spring ski trips in this part of the Coast Mountains, for which we used boats to access the icefields. On the one hand it seems totally appropriate to a landscape so intimately intertwined with water, but on the other it always seems pretty odd that you can access a ski trip with a boat.

At the beginning of May 2009, we left behind the blossoms of Vancouver and made the long drive north to still-snowbound Telegraph Creek on the banks of the Stikine River. Together with Gord Ferguson, Stan Sovdat, Mark Grist, Warren Wright, Don Jardine and Gord Bose, our plan was to ski across the glaciers between the Stikine and Iskut Rivers. To reach the start of our trip we were hoping to canoe 30 km down the Stikine River, which would take us deep into the mountains on its path to the coast. Ironically we had to wait for breakup on the river. We needed snow in the mountains but we didn't want ice on the river.

We launched from the remains of a dock that steamships had used up until the late 1960s. Chunks of ice still lined the riverbanks. The leafless branches of willow and poplar gave the surrounding hillsides a desolate appearance, but opening leaf

Right: John gets refreshing, cold water from a side stream on Sphaler Creek. *LB*

Below: Mark Grist and Warren Wright relax in their tent after a full day of skiing. *JB*

buds added a hint of green. Strong winds whipped against the fast current, threatening to tip our canoes and kayaks. Being on the water was a good way to slowly release our ties with civilization.

Downstream from Yehiniko Creek we left the river, on foot at first but quickly switching to skis. We followed a rough trail that climbed up into the main valley of Yehiniko Creek. This was one of the broad, U-shaped interior valleys that over the next three days slowly led us up into the mountains. Finally at the head of the valley we skied up a gentle glacier, which led us up to a col that was like a gateway to a different world. Peaks jutted out from between layers of mist as we transitioned into the glaciated landscape that we would follow for the next two weeks.

Quiet nights and corn snow. That is mostly how it was except for the snoring; three tents high on the glaciers of the northern Coast Mountains. Day after day we moved south through this serene landscape. The terrain was perfect for travel on skis: long glaciers threaded their way through steep mountains and each river of ice connected to the next. A side trip gave us views of the sheer northeast face of Ambition Mountain, while another gave us glimpses of the high summits west of the Stikine River.

Above: Road building equipment sits abandoned in previously untouched Sphaler Creek. *JB*

Opposite bottom: Making our way around crevasses while descending into Sphaler Creek valley. *LB*

The crux of our trip was crossing a pass southwest of Mount Hickman. The south side of the col was a tumbling icefall that had to be skirted by side-slipping down a 40-degree slope. Strapping our crazy carpet toboggans onto the tops of our heavy packs added to our apprehension as we slid over the first roll at the top of the 200 m slope. The first pitch, above some rocks, was exposed. Below that we could switch from side-slipping to smooth, controlled turns, and once past the crux we were rewarded with silky turns that lasted for 4 km down a glacier.

We spent several days travelling through the next conglomeration of glaciers. Big open slopes offered ideal spring skiing. One slope was so good that we were enticed to do three runs on the smooth corn snow. From a peak south of Mount Hickman we got a view of the most stunning contrast between the brown, dirt-scarred headwaters of Schaft Creek to the northeast and the glistening white maze of glaciated summits to the southwest. All of the glaciers had high trim lines along their lower reaches, marking how high the glaciers had once been. Many of the glaciers had lost over 100 m of ice since the 1970s.

Leaving this group of glaciers, we had another long easy ski down into the head of Sphaler Creek. About a kilometre past the snout of the glacier we emerged onto a snow-covered road. We were shocked to see a road in the midst of this remote wilderness. It was part of an 87 km long mining road that was being built to access the proposed Galore Creek mine. The planned road would slice through seven major tributaries of the Stikine watershed to reach right into the heart of this untouched

Pages 124–125: Looking west across Hoodoo Glacier to Surprise Mountain. *LB*

wilderness. Piles of culverts and an excavator and grader were left there for work on the road. But they were not waiting for spring. The road had been started several years earlier and the developer was in such a rush that it was being built in sections. Heavy-lift helicopters had been used to fly in the machines. The price of minerals had since dropped and now the road and all the equipment had been abandoned.

The road we were standing on led nowhere; it connected to nothing. It was disturbing to see this pure wilderness in the process of being ripped open. Thankfully the road had been temporarily suspended—but for how long?

The entire wilderness region that encompasses the Stikine, Iskut and Spatsizi Rivers is under threat from more than half a dozen large-scale industrial projects ranging from hydroelectric development to open-pit mines. This is a rare and irreplaceable wilderness—one of the few intact wilderness areas left in North America, and the kind of precious wilderness that no longer exists in any other part of the world. The presence of natural resources in this wilderness area makes it very vulnerable to the forces of development. Our resource-hungry civilization has been quick to exploit such regions as it has marched across North America, colliding with the natural land-

A rare sight—we were extremely lucky to glimpse this wolverine sprinting down the glacier past our camp on the Andrei Icefield. *LB*

scape. As Henry David Thoreau wrote in the 1800s, "Most men, it seems to me, do not care for nature and would sell their share in all her beauty for a given sum." In British Columbia it seems we cannot develop fast enough.

Heartbroken by what we saw in Sphaler Creek, we continued south to discover the Andrei Icefield. As we were cooking dinner that evening a wolverine raced down the glacier, passing within 200 m of our camp. We were lucky—it is rare to see these elusive animals. Even biologists who study wolverines seldom ever get to see them. Higher on the icefield we were hit with our first storm of the trip. Miraculously, especially for the north coast, the storm was short-lived and we were pinned down for only one day; the following day we moved to the south end of the icefield. From our last high camp on the Twin Glacier we made two side trips. First to a high peak to the west where we got sweeping views of the entire region, all the way from Ambition Mountain near the start of our trip to the rugged summits of Kates Needle and Burkett Needle on the huge icefield on the west side of the Stikine River. Our last climb was the broad snow dome of Hoodoo Mountain, an extinct volcano. From the edge of the summit we could see down 1,500 m to the Iskut River. After three weeks on these

A pair of bald eagles fly up the valley on our return trip up the Stikine River by jet boat. *JB*

Pages 128–129: John skis across
a frozen glacial lake near Hoodoo
Mountain. *LB*

vast icefields we appreciated how delicate the thin green valley was, in the midst of the ice-age landscape.

We left behind our snowy world and descended the Twin Glacier, dropping down into the lush depths of the Iskut River valley. The sudden return to the smell of the forest, the sound of running water and the warmth of the ground is always overwhelming after weeks spent on the glaciers. We camped on the riverbank that night with a fire and millions of stars glittering overhead. We had completed our ski trip but were still deep in the mountains. Though the goal of the trip was to complete the ski traverse, the real focus was just to soak up the wilderness.

Our last morning was the first time in weeks we didn't have to lug around our packs. Waves of peace flowed over us while we lounged in the sun waiting for the jet boat to pick us up. Dan Pakula eventually arrived with the jet boat and we piled in with skis and packs. Downstream the river widened and numerous braided channels fanned out over the flat valley bottom. It is here we learned about jet boats. When they are moving fast and planing, they draw only a few centimetres of water but as soon as they slow down to manoeuvre or avoid a logjam they instantly drop into the water and need a depth of 60 cm to avoid hitting the bottom. Dan had some trouble determining which of the many braided channels he should take to reach us and now, navigating back down the river fully loaded, he missed the correct channel. We ended up in a channel that drained over a shallow gravel bar and the boat got stuck.

Thinking this was routine, Gord asked Dan, "What do you normally do when this happens?" After a pause Dan replied, "This has never happened before."

The eight of us jumped off into the frigid knee-deep water, unloaded most of our gear and lined the boat around into a deeper channel. Dan breathed a big sigh of relief when we eventually got moving again and made it through the last of the shallows. The rest of our seven-hour jet boat ride took us through the some of the most stunning wilderness anywhere, first down the Iskut River and then back up the Stikine River to Telegraph Creek. Jagged snow-capped peaks rose 3,000 m above us and glaciers spilled down almost to the river. On our right the entire way back was the exceptional region we had just spent the last twenty-one days skiing through.

Stikine Icefield

Yes, we climb Fuji, but the purpose is not to "conquer" it, but to be impressed with its beauty, grandeur and aloofness. If we succeed in climbing a high mountain, why not say, "We have made a good friend of it?"
—Daisetz Suzuki

Our boat ride back up the Stikine River at the end of our Iskut trip was so inspiring that we started to conjure up plans to come back to explore the mountains and icefields on the west side of the river. As we were passing the Flood Glacier we came up with the idea to ski across the Stikine Icefield from the west and exit by coming down the Flood Glacier to the river. A little research showed that one of the few people to

View of Stikine Icefield with the iconic Devils Thumb peak dominating the skyline. *JB*

take skis up the Flood Glacier was Fred Beckey, who made the first ascent of the Devils Thumb in 1947 using this approach. By chance, we met Fred Beckey that summer in Bella Coola and over dinner we asked him about the Flood Glacier. Needless to say, the glacier has changed so much that it didn't really matter what his answer was.

So in April 2012, along with Stan Sovdat, Gord Ferguson and Dan Carey, we boarded the Alaska ferry in Bellingham, commencing another journey north to the Stikine. The two-day journey north to Petersburg was a relaxing way to start the trip as the ferry wove through a maze of mist-shrouded islands into the cold, driving rain of the north coast. On one of the scheduled stops we disembarked in Ketchikan and were greeted by a giant wooden "rain gauge" reaching its way more than a storey up the side of a building, graphically illustrating what the annual precipitation of 3.9 m looked like.

In Petersburg we waited through several days of rainy weather, peering across Frederick Sound in the direction of the mountains. Watching the movement of the tides and wind on the water, we spotted whales, sea lions, icebergs and a brief

Right: Unloading packs and skis in Thomas Bay, with Baird Glacier in the background. *JB*

Below: Roped up for safety while skiing through a heavily crevassed section of the North Baird Glacier. *JB*

glimpse of Devils Thumb shrouded in swirling clouds 45 km away. Erupting out of the heart of the Stikine Icefield, Devils Thumb is one of the most striking summits in the Coast Mountains and is one of the key peaks we hoped to get close to on our trip. After four days, a break in the weather opened up long enough for us to put in our food cache by helicopter.

At last we loaded our gear into Scott Hurley's aluminum charter boat and set off across Frederick Sound. Scott dropped us off at Thomas Bay, a mere 200 m from the Baird Glacier. The lower reaches of the glacier were snow free so we strapped on our crampons to cross the frozen ocean of ice, climbing up and down over massive pressure ridges and winding through a maze of crevasses. The sky was black with moisture-laden clouds and dark green rainforest grew up the steep slopes above the sides of the glacier. We turned left onto the North Baird Glacier and made it 6 km before setting up our first camp on the bare ice a mere 180 m above sea level.

In the morning we reached snow and switched to skis, still within sight of the ocean. For the next few kilometres we wove our way in and out of massive crevasses that split the glacier. Mist-shrouded cliffs and icefalls lined the sides of the grey corridor of ice. At 700 m the clouds descended and we were pinned down for a day by heavy rain, with temperatures just above freezing.

Local mountaineer Dieter Klose describes the Stikine Icefield as "one wet, sodden place." It was a wet winter in Petersburg that year, with over 3 m of precipitation. By applying the normal rule of thumb that 1 cm of precipitation equals 10 cm of snow, that translated to over 30 m of snowfall on the icefield for the winter. We hoped the weather patterns that made the winter so wet would not continue.

Rain eased on the afternoon of the fourth day and we made a push to get to the airdrop, skiing 16 km up the gentle glacier. Trail-breaking in the snowstorm was heavy work and even using the GPS it was hard to find the food cache, as it was nearly buried. It had snowed over a metre since Stan placed the food cache six days earlier, and the bamboo stakes marking the cache were now just barely sticking out of the snow. The next day we were hit by another snowstorm.

Our camp by the food cache was in a broad gentle pass between the head of the North Baird Glacier and a tributary of the massive Dawes Glacier. At 1,400 m we would be well below treeline in many mountain ranges, but here we were camped in a landscape dominated by ice. With only 25 km to the ocean in either direction, seagulls passed by regularly on their route between the inlets.

From the food cache we turned east and handrailed our way along the base of the steep flank of peaks at the southern edge of the Dawes Glacier. The glacier appeared

Silty multi-hued glacial meltwater makes patterns on the surface of the Baird Glacier. *JB*

Pages 134–135: With crampons on our ski boots, we make our way through pressure waves of ice on the Baird Glacier. This is typical weather in Alaska. Thomas Bay is visible behind. *JB*

Above: Higher up on the North Baird Glacier we struggle to navigate in a snowstorm to find our food cache. *LB*

Right: John peeks out of the partly-buried tent to look for signs of the weather clearing. *JB*

even more enormous in scale due to the unsettled weather, with distant peaks coming and going between clouds, mist and swirling snow. We were awed by the huge quantities of ice pouring off every slope. After two days we made it to a broad pass between the Dawes and Baird Glaciers. We arrived in a snowstorm, unable to see anything. The wind had shifted to the east and our instincts told us that the unsettled weather of the last few days was about to be replaced by a big storm.

For the next three days our world shrunk to two tents surrounded by swirling snow in a completely white landscape. It snowed constantly and we needed to shovel out the tents several times a day to prevent being totally buried. Such is life on an icefield. For entertainment we piled into the bigger tent for afternoon card games. By the end of the storm we were wallowing under 2 m of new snow.

The storm ended abruptly with a cold clear morning and we eagerly set off to explore the peaks that were invisible to us during the storm. We broke trail through boot-top powder towards a 2,562 m summit northeast of camp. Weaving past a few seracs we skied up onto the final shoulder before kicking steps up the last steep pitch to the summit. To the north, the sheer face of Mount Ratz towered above us, while southward, the icefield dazzled in the sun. It was a jaw-dropping view: we could see the long smooth tributaries of the Baird Glacier coming together as they turned west to the sea, and out of all this ice rose Devils Thumb, Cats Ears and Mount Burkett,

Devils Thumb is one of the most spectacular peaks in the Coast Mountains. This photo shows a rare glimpse of the many-times-sought but yet-unclimbed 1800 m north face. *JB*

Pages 138–139: Glacial ice gives this striking pool of meltwater its deep blue colour. The next day the glacier had shifted and the pool was gone. *LB*

some of the most spectacular sharp rock spires imaginable. Our map showed that our summit was almost on the Canada–US border but the concept of a border seemed so foreign in the ice-covered landscape. From our viewpoint it was hard to imagine that there really were other people on this continent besides us. The 700 m descent was boot-top powder, not bad for mid-May. In the afternoon we skied to another subpeak southwest of camp for a closer view of Devils Thumb. It was one of those sublime days that you hope will never end, but as we returned to camp, clouds were covering the western sky and by bedtime it was snowing again.

With less than a week of food left we were still not yet at the halfway point on our traverse. It had snowed nine out of the past eleven days and after much deliberation

over what to do we decided to abandon our plans to cross the icefield and instead return back the way we came. Over the next few days we meandered our way across the glaciers and skied back down the North Baird Glacier. At times we struggled through heavy snow squalls with marginal visibility; other times we were treated to long shafts of sunlight hitting the snow-plastered peaks and huge, wide-open spaces. The weather was never quite good enough for another side trip, however, so we pushed on, hoping to reach Thomas Bay before heavy rain returned.

Once below the snow line, we camped on the bare ice beside azure blue pools of meltwater on the glacier. By morning the glacier had shifted and the ponds had disappeared. This lower part of the glacier had receded dramatically, losing 180 m of

Above: John checks the map as we navigate back down the Dawes Glacier in a whiteout. *LB*

Left: Dan Carey skis off Peak 2562 m with the high peaks of the Stikine Icefield as a backdrop, including Devils Thumb and the stunning Cats Ears spires on the left. *JB*

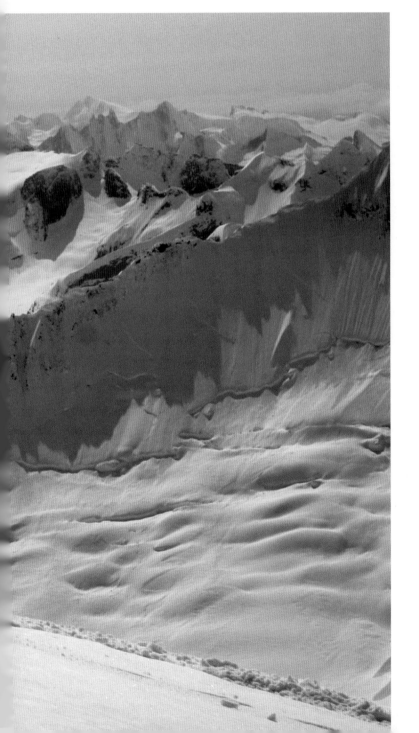

Opposite: John leaps across a crevasse on our way back down the North Baird Glacier. *LB*

Two small figures add scale to the sea of ice on the lower Baird Glacier. *JB*

ice in the last twenty or thirty years. It likely wouldn't be long before the North Baird Glacier no longer reached the main Baird Glacier.

As we cramponed our way down the bare ice, the ocean came into view—while we were still 6 km from the toe of the glacier. Lower down we could actually smell the ocean, that thick coastal smell that reminds us more of kayak trips than of being on a glacier. At Thomas Bay we camped on a moss-covered gravel bar within sight of the glacier terminus. Our campsite was buried under metres of ice until not long ago, and in the 1880s the glacier was large enough to calve icebergs into the ocean. We wondered why the forest had not reclaimed the gravel flats and later learned that the main Baird Glacier produces huge outburst floods from a glacial-dammed lake every dozen or so years. Each flood sends a massive 15 m wall of water across the gravel flats and out into Thomas Bay. The slow motion of the glaciers tends to mask the dynamic nature of this sensational landscape.

Above: Rare and unusual balls of moss known as "glacier mice." The moss starts growing around clumps of sand or small rocks and as the glacier melts, the masses slowly roll around like tumbleweed to form round balls. *LB*

Right: Linda poses on an iceberg calved from the Le Conte Glacier. The Le Conte Glacier, visible in the background, is the southernmost tidewater glacier in the northern hemisphere. *JB*

We weren't sure what to make of being back at our starting point in Thomas Bay. On the one hand we had struggled with the bad weather and hadn't completed our planned traverse, but in a different way the trip was still a huge success. We had gotten an intimate glimpse of the huge glaciers, from their snow-drenched summits to the crumbling ice at their snouts.

Eric Yancey arrived with his charter jet boat to take us back to Wrangell. But on our boat ride back to civilization he first took us to see the Le Conte Glacier, the southernmost tidewater glacier in the northern hemisphere. As we rounded the entrance to Le Conte Bay it looked like any other small coastal inlet with dark green rainforest rising from the water's edge, except for one thing: there was the odd iceberg bobbing about. We passed more and more icebergs, and soon realized the entire bay was jammed full of them. From here we could see the Le Conte Glacier, its sea of broken ice cascading down out of the mountains and ending in a jagged wall of turquoise blue ice at the head of the bay. As we watched, huge towers of ice cracked and fell into the sea. The glacier originates on the south side of Devils Thumb, 45 km from the ocean, and because we had just come from the same place we felt connected to the chunks of ice floating in the bay.

After three weeks of camping on snow, John relaxes on the soft moss-covered ground upon our return to Thomas Bay. *LB*

We had an extra day in Wrangell before our ferry so Eric took us in his jet boat up the lower reaches of the Stikine River to soak in the wooden barrel at Chief Shakes Hot Springs. As we jetted our way up the river, Eric explained that the entire lower portion of the river that is in Alaska is protected as part of the Stikine–Le Conte Wilderness. We thought of our previous trip in the upper part of the Stikine in Canada and recalled the devastation happening there—what a contrast. As Canadians we are often quick to blame the US for destroying their wilderness, yet in the Stikine the opposite is happening. The Alaska Panhandle is home to the Taku, Whiting, Iskut-Stikine, Unuk and Nass Rivers. From tidewater to their glacial headwaters, these watersheds are largely intact, globally significant wilderness. And ironically all of them are threatened by large-scale industrial projects on the British Columbia side of the border. With the gift of having some of the most amazing pieces of wilderness left on the planet, we have some urgent questions to answer. Are they ours to destroy or do we have a responsibility to protect them?

CHAPTER EIGHT:

TOUCH THE WILD

It is a commonplace of all religious thought, even the most primitive,

that the man seeking visions and insight must go apart from his

fellows and live for a time in the wilderness.

— Loren Eiseley

Pages 146–147: Diana Diaconu and Gord Ferguson stroll along a creek draining into Atlin Lake. *JB*

Marina Dodis beside a small tarn above Princess Louisa Inlet at dusk, with Mount Albert in the background. *LB*

Throughout human history, wilderness has provided a place of solace and comfort, a place of spiritual renewal. Its timelessness and scale provide a perspective that restores a sense of balance and completeness to us as we live our busy lives. Lying on the mossy floor of the forest, swimming in alpine pools and climbing high onto icefields, we have come to feel part of the wilderness.

The experience of wilderness has many aspects to it. There are the physical challenges of lugging a heavy pack up mountainsides, and the discomforts of cold and sweat, as well as the thrills of standing on a high peak or skiing off its narrow summit, or the sense of peace that comes from the searing beauty and the silence of the mountains. Here, at the boundary between inner and outer landscapes, is where our relationship with the wilderness exists, where maps form dreams and landscape is understood through imagination. And it is here that we begin to touch the wilderness.

Above: Fluted snow ridges on peaks in Alaska. *LB*

Left: Close-up of a rainbow. *JB*

Maps and Dreams

There is a love of wild nature in everybody, an ancient mother-love showing itself whether recognized or no, and however covered by cares and duties.
—John Muir

If you were to sit at home and watch someone's progress on a long trip through the wilderness—as you can now literally do with GPS communication devices—you could see their track move across the landscape, up over passes, along ridge tops, down past lakes and through meadows. You could zoom in on satellite photos and get a glimpse of that azure blue lake they camped beside, the green meadows beyond it and the shape of the mountain above. You could maybe get a feel for what desires caused them to go in certain directions and take particular routes. Their path would be an expression of that person getting to know the landscape, a time-lapse drawing of their relationship to it, a kind of artwork etched on the landscape.

But what you wouldn't see are the flowers and trees, the rocks and patterns in the mud, the moon and the stars at night or the sudden encounters with grizzly bears and wolves. You wouldn't be able to feel the silky smooth water of the alpine tarns

Grizzly tracks contrast with patterns in dry mud. *JB*

Above: The Waddington Range is silhouetted against an evening sky. *LB*

Left: Drainage runnels on a weathered slope created dramatic patterns in Graveyard Creek. *LB*

Pages 152–153: Clouds rise from the surrounding valleys and lend a mysterious look to the landscape as this skier heads south across the Homathko Icefield. *JB*

151

Right: Plumes of snow whip across windy slopes after a snowstorm. *LB*

Below: Ascending Mount Queen Mary in the Saint Elias Mountains. Canada's highest summit, Mount Logan, is visible top right. *JB*

The sun glistens off icicles. *JB*

they swam in or the tingling on their skin from the cold water as they lay in the warm sun, drying in the wind. You wouldn't be able to feel their heavy breathing and the weight of their pack on their shoulders, or their boots and ankles trying to grip on the steep slopes. You wouldn't be able to feel the sense of peace that slowly grows in them or the warmth in their chest that is stirred up by the searing beauty of these wild places.

At some point you might start to wonder what it is that is guiding the adventurer you are tracking. What steers them—how did they plan their route, and how do they decide where to walk?

It often starts with a dream, poring over maps and satellite photos. Is it possible to cross that ridge? Is the glacier going to be crevassed? How long would it take to detour around that mountain? Is that flat area meadow or rock? Studying maps is the technical side of planning an extended trip in the wilderness. Contours, elevations, distances, slope angles. Figuring out the most efficient routes, campsites and viewpoints. Our left brains thrive on these sorts of technical details.

Dreams, on the other hand, guide the process. Our right brains wonder what the alpine flowers will smell like or what the view from the ridge will look like, or what the thundering of a waterfall will sound like. These emotions, images, ideas and aspirations fuel our dreams.

Joining these two perspectives—maps and dreams—is a creative process. It requires a playful curiosity about the landscape. You need to study the terrain and get to know it in all its aspects before you plan your route.

Access to the mountains sometimes requires hiking through rare stands of spectacular West Coast rainforest. *JB*

When we were young, mountains were our goal. And from the top of a mountain we would see another mountain that we would then want to climb and our ambition became to climb every mountain in sight. As we became interested in larger and larger areas of wilderness our dreams shifted from climbing a single mountain to seeing whole icefields and mountain ranges. In much the same way that a climber is drawn to an aesthetically appealing line on a mountain, we were drawn to large blank areas on maps, and figuring out routes through these regions became our goal.

To traverse a mountain range or cross an icefield became a new way to interact with the mountains. But we quickly came to realize that any goal is just a framework for getting to know the landscape. The rewards of the summits are not just in reaching the peaks or traversing an icefield but in the journey itself. It's about the process: the route or summit is a destination that forms the trip, but the real goal is being in the wilderness. For us, climbing mountains has always been more like being at the beach as a kid, lifting up barnacle-covered rocks to see what's under them. It's not that you expect to find anything but it's the looking—the exploring—that matters. It creates a spirit of discovery and gives you a sense of purpose that helps you to bound off enthusiastically into the mountains. Each trip in the wilderness is like spending time

Pages 158–159: John peers out across seracs on the Bute Glacier below the north face of Bute Mountain. *LB*

Late-summer seed pods of western anemone are silhouetted against the sun. *JB*

Descending the 75-km-long Kaskawulsh Glacier in the Saint Elias Mountains. *LB*

with someone you love. Slowly the many facets of their personality are revealed, and a deep bond develops. The wilderness becomes an experience rather than a place.

This spirit of discovery guides the planning process as well. To look at wilderness on the map, to really study it, and to dream about what it might be like. When you stare at detailed maps of wilderness areas you can sense that there is a kind of power in such raw, wild landscapes, and the desire to experience that vitality becomes one of the objectives of the trip. In the process it becomes important to honour that power. It is necessary to acknowledge that something like 4,000 square km of ice will seep into your bones over three weeks and make you see and appreciate things in a different way. The way to honour that power is to approach it with the right frame of mind—to be open to it, and to experience the wilderness first hand.

For us this often means walking across an entire intact wilderness region, if possible, even if this means bushwacking up difficult valleys. It is about considering a wilderness area as a whole. For instance, approaches are sometimes what really spell out how far into the wilderness you are. The bush is sometimes more wild and remote than the alpine. This creates a subtle shift in the process, from taking only what you want from the mountains to being open to all aspects of the wilderness.

So it's not just about getting that nice powder run off the peaks; it is equally about seeing the beauty when you are struggling up a wild valley or slogging across a flat icefield. Learning to accept, rather than judge or be selective, has been an important lesson for us and has helped us to realize that each and every part of the mountains is equally as beautiful as any other.

Three skiers ascend into an abstract world of shapes and patterns in the snow. *JB*

Landscape and Imagination

The great rhythm of nature pervades everything, and man is woven into it with mind and body. Even his imagination does not belong so much to the realm of the individual as to the soul of the landscape, in which the rhythm of the universe is condensed into a melody of irresistible charm.
—Lama Anagarika Govinda

JOHN'S JOURNAL: On a trip to the Pantheon Range a few years ago, I remember making a connection that made me realize how important imagination is in relating to the landscape. I had a flashback to when my kids were young and how they played with action figures on the beach, climbing their characters over logs and past tide pools.

I remembered doing the same thing as a child, moving my action figures past fluted rocks and weathered pieces of driftwood, exploring the wonderful things only a kid could find at the beach. I had outgrown the action figures, but now here I was moving myself through the landscape, exploring these incredible mountains—not as an adult but as an action figure attached to the arm of a child drawn to smooth shapes, jagged edges and sparkles in the snow. Only now the action figure has been replaced by my heart and the goal is to feel and sense everything about the landscape with passion.

Imagination is how we interpret our perceptions and determine our overall experience of landscape. Imagination is the creative process needed to know a landscape and understand the significance of the ordinary world. As Albert Einstein said, "Imagination is more important than knowledge. Knowledge is limited. Imagination encircles the world."

What is it that sparks our imagination? Every place has a different feeling and energy to it: wild windswept ridge tops, quiet mossy glades, a tangle of slide alder and devil's club, the riot of colour in alpine flowers, or the Japanese garden–like details of a babbling creek. These are the things that tug at the strings attached to our hearts, the things that guide our souls. Being in the wilderness is about moving your soul over the landscape, and using your imagination to connect with it through your heart.

Opposite: A western hemlock silhouetted against a waterfall. *JB*

Indian hellebore leaves create a complex pattern. *JB*

In this way one can get to know the land and move with the flow of the land. Through imagination we can feel the landscape and let that guide us. Imagination is like a form of internal compass that we use to navigate the landscape. We use our experience of landscape to guide us through openings in the forest or to find the natural routes of travel over a ridge, or to find a sheltered spot to camp. It is also a way of developing some sense of how the world is—of feeling both the power and the stillness of a mountain, the tranquility and vitality of a river, and the sublime.

Imagination is also about the feeling of being one with nature. But to truly imagine a landscape, one must go beyond fear and beyond conflict with nature. We have to be willing to accept the wilderness as it is, not as we would like it to be. This is not about taking from or controlling the wilderness, it is about listening to its utter silence.

It's often unclear when a trip in the wilderness ends. Sometimes you are standing at the edge of the water on a beach when you realize you are no longer in the land of the giants. Other times you feel as though you are still somewhere up on a mountaintop where you belong. Sometimes this feeling lasts for a while, sometimes it doesn't. When you are back in civilization it's hard to stay with the wild; we are drawn back into the busy world of thought that dominates our culture—the technical details of living in our complex society. But sometimes when you get caught up in it all, you pause and imagine what it might be like high up on some icefield right now, or to be deep in a grove of old growth with the moss glowing its fluorescent green.

Being in the wilderness strips away all the man-made fabrications and the veneer of civilization we carry through our lives. The day of the week, names, the way we see ourselves, even words are no longer relevant, and we are taken to a simpler elemental connection with how we really are. The wilderness has the power to change the posture of our consciousness.

Opposite: Lars Wilke takes in the serene beauty of Alsek Lake. *LB*

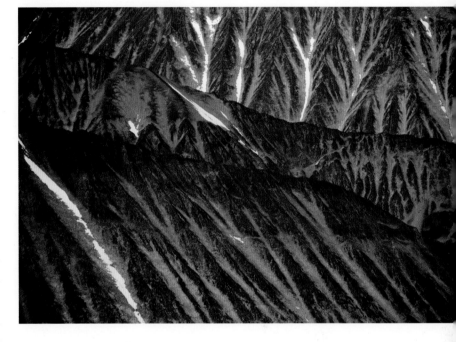

Ridge patterns seen from the summit of Mount Vic in the South Chilcotin Mountains. *JB*

CHAPTER NINE:

SOUL OF WILDERNESS

In the point of rest at the center of our being, we encounter a world where all things are at rest in the same way. Then a tree becomes a mystery, a cloud a revelation, each man a cosmos of whose riches we can only catch glimpses. The life of its simplicity is simple, but it opens to us a book in which we never get beyond the first syllable.

—Dag Hammarskjöld

Pages 166–167: A small figure is dwarfed by this big-sky sunset. *JB*

Mist and clouds shroud the lofty peaks in the Saint Elias Range. *LB*

When you travel slowly through the mountains day after day, week after week, you realize that behind the thunder of falling seracs and the roar of waterfalls there is a powerful silence, and you begin to feel the beauty and rhythm of this wilderness deep within your soul. You feel the energy of the wilderness inside of you, filling your whole being. There is a feeling of joy and an awareness of the miracle of life. It's as if the wilderness—its life, its soul—is actually within us. Part of the wilderness is in us and we are part of it. Without any concrete thought we come to believe that the wild summits and icefields are alive, that the earth is alive. Not walking, talking alive, but they have a spirit, a soul.

For us, it was not a thought, it was a feeling deep inside—something we felt with our own souls. This feeling grew stronger over the years. At first we didn't think anything of it. It was not something we could explain to anybody. That would be like trying to assign human ways to animals: all of us as schoolchildren, writers and editors are taught not to anthropomorphize, but when you watch a raven playing in the wind you know they are having fun. And the suggestion that the wilderness has a soul is such a preposterous idea in our Western culture.

Partly unsure of ourselves, and partly wondering how you would explain it, we became curious to know what others believed about the soul of wilderness. We began to read what people had to say about their most intimate relationship with the earth. We started with *Touch the Earth* and *The Way of the Earth* by T.C. McLuhan. We were bolstered by what we read about cultures spanning the centuries from around the world: Native North America, Australian Aboriginals, eastern philosophies of Zen, Buddhism and Hinduism, people from Africa, and even the English romantic poets of the nineteenth century all spoke of the soul of the earth.

Our first confirmation was from our own North American First Nations, who we see as our spiritual leaders in reconnecting with the earth. Bill Tallbull, a Northern Cheyenne, wrote: "When Indian people walk down the valley, they have had a spiritual relationship, a spiritual tie with the area." Robert Blackcoat, a Navajo elder,

Skiers are framed by billowing clouds on the Juneau Icefield. *JB*

Pages 170–171: Wolverine tracks wind their way through shadows in the high alpine. The tracks were left raised above the snow surface after wind eroded the surrounding snow. *JB*

169

Opposite: Deep freshly fallen snow created this dramatic pattern of curves along the banks of Cerise Creek. *LB*

stated: "We are taught that everything is alive. It is hard to teach somebody else that the land is alive." Similarly, Sister Mary José Hobday wrote, "Not only do Indians love the land because it mingles with the dust of the dead, but because it is vital and alive, and is part of the life of each person."

These ideas were also found in many other cultures. In reference to Australian Aboriginals, T.C. McLuhan wrote, "Land is the basis of Aboriginal life. It is also the umbilical cord to the soul." While in Japan, thirteenth-century Zen master Dogen Kigen wrote, "The ocean speaks and mountains have tongues—that is the everyday speech of Buddha." More recently, Zen teacher Daisetz Suzuki wrote, "The spirit of the earth breathes at the innermost recesses of the individual."

And according to ancient Hindu scriptures of the Vedanta in the Isa Upanishad, "This entire cosmos, whatever is still or moving, is pervaded by the divine." While in the writings of Amadou Hampâté Bâ from Mali, "Earth is thought of as a living being." The nineteenth-century Romantic poet William Wordsworth spoke of "one interior life that lives in all things."

More recently, William O. Douglas, an associate justice of the Supreme Court of the United States, noted that "To be whole and harmonious, man must also know the music of the beaches and the woods. He must find the thing of which he is only an infinitesimal part and nurture it and love it, if he is to live."

These observations made us feel like we weren't crazy after all. But we wondered how you would explain the concept to someone. It is not something you can explain rationally; it is something you have to feel in your heart. And yet we kept wondering how we could make it easier to understand.

Strong winds etch patterns in snow, similar to eroded mountains. *JB*

Opposite: A skier enters a striking landscape of strong light on snow-covered rocks. *LB*

JOHN'S JOURNAL: It was my mother who helped me reframe what soul might look like. It was one of the last things she taught me. My mother died of Alzheimer's disease. Like most terminal illnesses it is a terrible disease, and in my mother's case it saw her deteriorate gradually over seven years. For the later part of her time with this disease she was bedridden, unable to speak. During my regular visits I was unable to converse with her or communicate in a way that most people would consider meaningful. The functions of her brain had deteriorated to the point that she probably couldn't manage more than the most basic thoughts, yet I could still feel a connection with her. Her soul remained strong, and her eyes communicated that she appreciated the company. It was a totally new way to visit. There were no distractions from wayward thoughts and irrelevant conversation. I learned that if I took the time to just sit with her and not focus on my own thoughts, but be open to her, that we could have as good a visit as if we had had a long conversation. The visit became simply a pure awareness of the other person.

We ask you to consider the wilderness in this way. The earth has a soul. Like John visiting with his mother, you can relate to the earth's soul not by talking, thinking and interacting in the normal sense, but by being still and listening to the radiating silence. In this manner it is possible to connect with the wilderness—or rather to realize that you are already connected to it. And doing so is perhaps the only way we can make the wilderness part of our culture.

Play of light on the crystal-clear water of a high mountain lake. *LB*

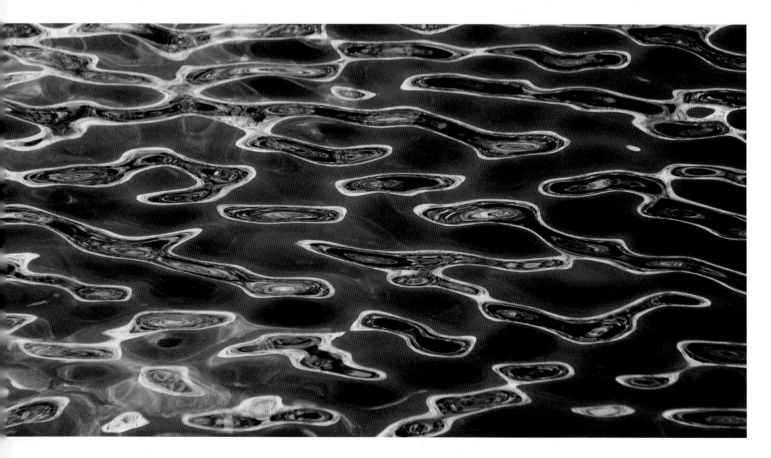

Harbour Publishing Co. Ltd.
P.O. Box 219, Madeira Park, BC, V0N 2H0
www.harbourpublishing.com

Edited by Pam Robertson
Text design and typesetting by Roger Handling
Map on page 6 by Roger Handling
Printed and bound in China

All photographs by John Baldwin (JB) and Linda Bily (LB)

Harbour Publishing acknowledges the support of the Canada Council for the Arts, which last year invested $157 million to bring the arts to Canadians throughout the country. We also gratefully acknowledge financial support from the Government of Canada through the Canada Book Fund and from the Province of British Columbia through the BC Arts Council and the Book Publishing Tax Credit.

Cataloguing data available from Library and Archives Canada
ISBN 978-1-55017-735-0 (cloth)

Grateful acknowledgement is made to the following authors and/or publishers for generously giving permission to reprint quotations from these copyrighted works:

Abbey, Edward. *Beyond the Wall: Essays from the Outside.* New York: Henry Holt and Company, 1984.

Baldwin, John. "Thirty Years on Ice," *Canadian Alpine Journal,* 2012.

Blackcoat, Robert. quoted in Anita Parlow. *Cry Sacred Ground.* Washington, DC: The Christic Institute, 1988.

Chadwick, Douglas. *The Wolverine Way.* Ventura: Patagonia Books, 2010.

Eiseley, Loren. *The Immense Journey.* New York: Random House, 1957.

Gmoser, Hans. "High Level Ski Route from Lake Louise to Jasper," *Canadian Alpine Journal,* 1961.

Govinda, Lama Anagarika. *The Way of the White Clouds.* New York: The Overlook Press, 2005.

Hobday, Sister Mary Jose. "Seeking a Moist Heart," *Western Spirituality.* ed. Matthew Fox, Rochester, VT: Bear and Co., 1981.

Hume, Mark. *Run of the River.* Vancouver: New Star Books, 1992.

Macfarlane, Robert. *Mountains of the Mind.* London: Granta Books, 2003.

McLuhan, T.C. *The Way of the Earth.* New York: Simon and Schuster, 1994.

Snyder, Gary. *The High Sierra of California.* Berkeley: Heydey Books, 2005.

Suzuki, Daisetz. *Japanese Spirituality.* Westport: Greenwood Press, 1988.

Suzuki, Daisetz. *Zen and Japanese Culture.* Princeton: Princeton University Press, 1989.

Tallbull, Bill. "On the Tongue River Valley," *Proceedings of the National Sacred Sites Caucus,* Association on American Indian Affairs, 1991.